a better life

100 ATHEISTS SPEAK OUT ON
JOY & MEANING
IN A WORLD WITHOUT GOD

CHRIS JOHNSON

A BETTER LIFE: 100 ATHEISTS SPEAK OUT ON JOY & MEANING IN A WORLD WITHOUT GOD

First Edition, December 2013

ISBN-13: 978-0-9899360-0-2
ISBN-10: 0989936007

www.theatheistbook.com
chris@theatheistbook.com

Printed in South Korea.

TABLE OF CONTENTS

INTRODUCTION
BY CHRIS JOHNSON, PHOTOGRAPHER

The White Sands National Monument in New Mexico is a vast expanse of sand dunes which stretches out against the backdrop of the San Andres Mountains. The sand looks like snow, and it's all you can see in every direction. It feels like you're standing on another planet. It's a breathtaking experience. White Sands is one of the most beautiful places I have ever been.

I first visited the park with my brother, taking in the exquisite scenery while on a road trip from Texas to our home state of Washington. Our route followed some of the most stunning vistas in the country, from the Grand Canyon to Yellowstone National Park.

Visiting these natural treasures, I was struck with how lucky I am to be able to experience them. The cosmic lottery we have all won by just being alive is something to cherish. As an atheist, these experiences are all the more poignant and meaningful because, as far as I know, this is the only life I'm going to get. This is not a dress rehearsal before ascending to heaven, nor a stop along the cosmic journey of experiences. This is it, and that makes a difference.

Through this book, I want to express the many and varied ways that atheists cherish the moments we get in this life. In addition, I want to explore how we cope with our mortality, and how, with no God to intervene, we are responsible for making the world a better place for ourselves, and those around us.

I also want to show the diversity within our community. We are from different countries, traditions, ethnicities, sexual orientations, and socio-economic backgrounds. We also have different ways that we label ourselves: atheists, non-theists, humanists, freethinkers, non-believers, brights, and more. Our one common factor is that that we don't believe in God.

Life is up to us, and it is quite a journey. There are moments of joy, and moments of pain and sorrow. We often don't fully appreciate what we have until it is gone. My hope is that this book can help us reflect on those we love as well as cherish the time we have together on this brief ride through life.

When we get to the end of our lives, we will hopefully have a body of experiences that we look back on fondly. As A.A. Milne wrote in *Winnie-the-Pooh*, "How lucky I am to have something that makes saying goodbye so hard."

Existence is fleeting, but how lucky we are to be here and experience all it has to offer, and to have the opportunity to make it a better life.

ALCHEMY
BY ANITA M. BARNARD

We are walking through a world of science,
wondrous mysteries and beautiful inquiries.

I hold the newborn kitten, the blooming
branch, my child's face, the tender
question in my cupped and perfect hands.

I hold the pen and try to capture
in my alchemy
of words
my joy and loss and awe at this
real world.

I hold my paintbrush and try
to express its inexpressible
beauty and allure.

We camp in the meadow.
The stars open up to me, and
we make love under the
forever of the night sky,
savoring its vast cold beauty, and
the warmth of the human, from inside the
orbit of my lover's arms.

I feel the celestial ballet.
All art is the mirror of science, of how
our world is painted. Vincent and
Galileo could see the stars dance.

We are dancing
here
with the butterflies and our brief seasons,
joining in the waltz of eternal circles with
the planets; not knowing, but asking;
not static, but always opening. Our minds,
our senses, and our sciences unfurl
like fingers, like flowers, open
their palms to us, offer us
their gifts.

Our flesh is the flesh
of the universe: stardust
as good a soul
as we will ever need.

a better life

ALEX HONNOLD
ROCK CLIMBER
SACRAMENTO, CALIFORNIA

In 2006, a friend and I first attempted to climb Freerider, a difficult route up Yosemite's El Capitan, one of the most impressive long routes in North America. At the time it was a bigger step forward in scope and difficulty than anything I'd previously climbed, and there were all the accompanying feelings of excitement and doubt that come from stepping out of your comfort zone. We climbed the route over a day and a half, one thousand feet up the wall the first afternoon, camping, and then climbing the more difficult upper two-thirds the following day.

We awoke early on our small granite ledge and started climbing immediately. There was nothing in our world but vertical rock above and below and we slowly worked our way higher. Over the course of the day clouds started building and by mid-afternoon, while we were still around five hundred feet from the top, we became enshrouded in swirling clouds and mist. We were inside the clouds; visibility dropped to nothing. We both worried about rain, but there was nothing to do but continue upward. As I led the final pitch to the summit I suddenly broke through the upper layer of clouds, revealing the whole Sierra Nevada, the so-called range of light, basking in the pink glow of sunset. To spend a whole day physically toiling, fearful and anxious about the weather and the difficult climbing, and then to break free from it all and top out amidst the most beautiful sunset of my life, the mountains wreathed in snow and the sun setting it all aflame with light— that is why I climb.

Since that day I've been lucky enough to become a professional rock climber. What started as small-scale sponsorships and free climbing gear has shifted into an actual profession that provides a living. Few people are fortunate enough to do for a living the one thing they love most; I'll always be grateful that I've settled into this life.

I find my purpose in pushing myself and exploring, constantly setting new goals and working towards them. I travel and climb full-time, always looking for the next big challenge or adventure. I find the whole process incredibly fulfilling, especially how it brings me into contact with the most beautiful parts of the natural world. Obviously it's not a life for everyone since it requires giving up many of the most comfortable parts of modern life like stability and a home. But for me, moments like the top of Freerider, moments of sublime beauty and connection with the world around me are well worth the trade.

Photos: climbing in Yosemite National Park

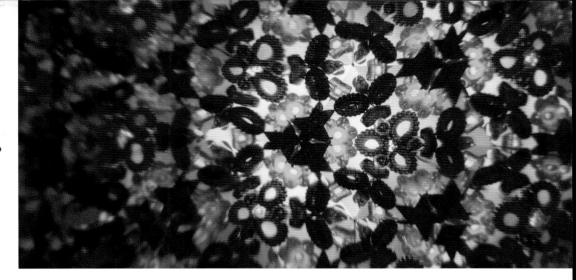

TRACIE HARRIS

CO-HOST, *GODLESS BITCHES* PODCAST,
THE ATHEIST EXPERIENCE
AUSTIN, TEXAS

[INTERVIEW] My husband asked me what I wanted for Christmas, and I said, "I really want a kaleidoscope." The reason I wanted one was—who doesn't love a kaleidoscope?

When you see one, you can't help but pick it up. You have to look at it. You have to see it. You can't just pass one up. It's like, "Oh, a kaleidoscope!" You want to see what's in there. "What happens when I turn it?" "What does it do?" "What kinds of colors or stones do you see?" There are some very expensive kaleidoscopes you can buy, and there are some very cheap ones; but it really doesn't matter. When you see one, you're almost compelled to pick it up because who doesn't feel the joy of all those colors moving and shifting, and those patterns. It's just beautiful. We have an aesthetic sense as human beings that makes us appreciate beautiful, fun things.

We did a thread one time on a social networking site I'm on, and talked about the idea of sprinkles. Sprinkles on ice cream or sprinkles on a cupcake, and how they're either, at best tasteless, or at worst, taste nasty. And yet, when you have something with or without sprinkles, everybody wants sprinkles, because they're so happy. They just bring happiness to the cupcake or to the ice cream. It's not a costly thing. It's just about the joy of the color. It's almost like eating confetti. Or eating a party!

People love things that they find beautiful. And it can be a very expensive thing or an exclusive thing, if somebody is a high-end connoisseur of something and appreciates some very expensive, valuable, rare, well-crafted piece of something. Or it can just be as simple as, "I used to have that when I was a child! And I can't believe I'm seeing this now in the thrift store! I haven't thought of this thing in thirty years!" And you just can't believe you're looking at this thing you used to love.

I just cannot imagine how anyone could go through life and avoid meaning or beauty, happiness, or love... Once you have the basic needs of your life met, there's really nothing left *but* to appreciate it.

NAHLA MAHMOUD

ENVIRONMENTALIST / HUMAN RIGHTS ACTIVIST
LONDON, UNITED KINGDOM

Reflecting on my journey as an ex-Muslim and an atheist, I can tell how privileged I am to have survived all the challenges I have been through and to have become the liberated person I am today. Growing up in an Islamic environment forced me to think about and question the unfairness and injustice of God from an early age. It became worse after puberty, since I was discriminated against as a woman according to gender-biased Islamic traditions. That, combined with my exposure to science and evidence-based thinking, made me resist and renounce Islam as a belief system.

Throughout my life, I have been particularly inspired by strong women—those who fought on the front lines and spoke out, demanding equal rights within the hostile male-dominant culture that exists in many regions. One of those women was my mother, who raised me along with my other four siblings after my dad passed away. She was an inspiration. She was a progressive, open-minded woman who challenged the dogma and conservative traditions widely practiced in the Sudanese community. Many other women—such as Simone de Beauvoir with her founding notions of contemporary feminism, Sudanese feminist Fatma Babikir with her contribution to modern African feminism, Egyptian writer Nawal el-Saadawi with her brilliant critiques of Islamisim, to name just a few—also served as role models throughout my journey.

My passion about nature and training as a scientist have also hugely influenced the way I think and see the world around me. Ever since I was a little girl at the age of seven, I have collected whatever caught my interest. My collection consisted of shiny stones, colorful beans, weird leaves, and many amazing insects which I

kept separately in a wooden box. Often before sunrise, I used to sit and enjoy watching the birds in our lovely garden with my grandfather. He lived nearby, so it was almost a daily habit that he stopped by our house to feed them with me.

I have vivid childhood memories of watching David Attenborough's *Africa* series, and excitedly learning about the continent's incredible wildlife. The great Charles Darwin was another major figure influencing my journey. I used to read about his work secretly, since the theory of evolution was and still is banned from the whole educational system. Shamefully, there is the punishment of jail for those who dare to speak about or teach it. However, I still enjoyed sneaking access to those forbidden books and materials online. I used to cover the "dangerous" hard copy ones with an external sheet and exchange them with friends in a dodgy way...lots of drama! After I graduated then from the University of Khartoum in Sudan, I spent some time in Tanzania before coming to the UK three years ago. Currently, I work as a research and development officer at an environmental organization in East London.

I often get asked about what I believe in and what motivates me if not God? Well, to put it simply, I am willing to make the best of this one life that I have. I enjoy exploring nature and its extraordinary beings on this beautiful planet. I feel privileged to live in an era of enlightenment, experiencing the joy of knowledge and discoveries. I greatly appreciate learning from and sharing knowledge with people around me. I hope for and look forward to influencing positive change, and making this world a better place for us and the coming generations.

I am up for this one life because I love puzzles, adore coffee, and enjoy good red wine served with blue cheese.

Photos: Eritrean coffee ceremony, London

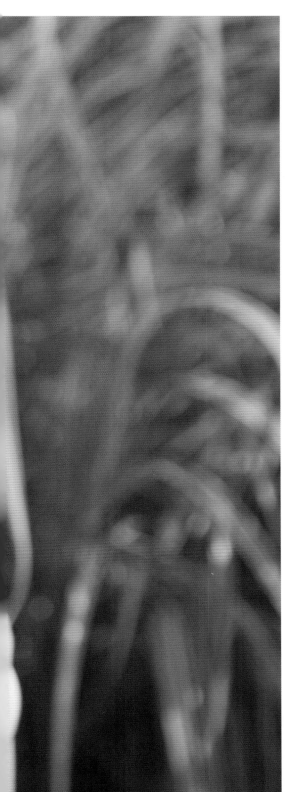

JULIA SWEENEY
ACTRESS / COMEDIAN / AUTHOR
CHICAGO, ILLINOIS

[INTERVIEW] Where do I find meaning? Sometimes I think religious theists have corrupted the meaning of *meaning*. At least, in the way the word is commonly used. Maybe "corrupted" is the wrong word. Co-opted. No! Hijacked. Yes, that's the word.

It's almost as if they've short-circuited the natural human inclination to desire meaning and context by having their followers memorize an answer. Something like: Your life has meaning because God created you and looks over you and puts obstacles in your path in order to see if your choices merit a life after death in bliss. Whenever that desire for meaning comes up, the theist's answer is already there. In fact, the answer is there even before the desire rears its existential head.

But the truth is, the religious find meaning in their lives in the same places I do: in family, in purposefulness, in friends and community, in the quest to understand better and to gain greater skill, in the desire to manipulate my circumstances and community (for better or worse).

Personally, right now—and my reservoir for meaning changes shape and substance there and again—I find meaning in: raising my daughter with my husband; in my ongoing relationships with my daughter and my husband, which increase in intimacy and understanding (although of course those relationships are filled with ups and downs too); in my increasingly knowledgeable understanding of how the world works; in my experiences with others' art; and mostly from my work writing. In regards to writing, I'm in a transition right now in my vocation. After years of performing on stage I'm turning myself towards writing exclusively. I can't say I'll never do a stage show again, but for right now I'm enthusiastic in my desire to learn how to write better and to practice and maintain habits that will allow for greater skill. I also find profound meaning in the small things like taking care of my body and my house. I find meaning in being present.

When I became an atheist, I felt lost for a while. I felt wobbly. I didn't know how I would integrate my new view of myself as a vulnerable being in a world of whim. But after a while, the understanding of my particularly small place in the natural order of life deepened, and my appreciation for this short stint—to be alive and aware—was activated. I was in thrall to this truth. This feeling has never left me. I've experienced much more moment-to-moment appreciation and meaning in my life as a result.

Looking back, it was as if my theistic worldview had numbed me. My natural worldview animated my senses. And I mean "sense" in all the ways one can use the word.

Frankly, it was the most profound experience of my life.

Below: Sweeney with her daughter Mulan

JAMES O'MALLEY
EDITOR, *THE POD DELUSION*
LONDON, UNITED KINGDOM

When asked to write about what brings me joy, my first thought was the most obvious one: my wonderful girlfriend, Liz. However, being both British and uptight, I find talking about feelings rather squeamish.

So instead I'd like to talk about something else that brings me joy: arguing.

Now this may seem counterintuitive—after all, how can you possibly derive joy from the act of people shouting at one another? I think there's an odd sort of beauty to it.

If you look back at history, you can see a great and continuous debate in which slowly but surely the many characters have battled both physically and intellectually, to give us the world as we conceptualize it today.

Three hundred and fifty years ago you had to be whatever religion the state told you to be—until early thinkers gave us a sniff of what would lead to secularism. Only three hundred years ago monarchy was seen as the default form of

a government—until Thomas Paine came along and explained why that was a bit silly. Only one hundred years ago women weren't allowed to vote—until the radical thinkers of the day realized this was stupid, too.

These battles of ideas were not won overnight but they demonstrate a progress of sorts, and a direct throughline can be drawn all the way to today in many contemporary debates: over gay marriage; access to abortion; and the conflict between the public square, privacy, and free speech. When viewed on a historical timescale—it seems victory for the positions held by rationalists and secularists are an inevitability, even when we face powerful entrenched interests defending the status quo.

And all of that history has left us where we are today: a far-from-perfect but free society able to debate ideas without risk of persecution. And this is something to be celebrated.

What's more is that, perhaps most importantly, these ideas have been underwritten and in many cases defined by advances in science. What's

brilliant about science is that it provides an even clearer mechanism for visible progress. The story of science shows constant progress—unlike political progress, which you can backslide under a tyrannical regime, it's relatively difficult (though not impossible) to forget that the earth orbits the sun—or how to make a printing press. And as time goes on, the total sum of our knowledge about the universe and how it works will keep increasing and keep creating more nuanced and fascinating challenges to the current order, and will force us to review, update, and improve the values and morals by which we live.

So drawn together, science and freethinking form a world view that is nicely coherent in its inability to stay the same. This means that whilst religious people when challenged with new ideas may feel threatened or wracked with doubt, I instead view the challenge with excitement—and an opportunity to ask questions and debate.

Also: Liz brings me lots of joy.

LIZ LUTGENDORFF
DEPUTY EDITOR, *THE POD DELUSION*
LONDON, UNITED KINGDOM

When I was younger, I thought being an adult would involve going to lectures and always being interested in things. I lived in the countryside and wanted to move to a city where I imagined there would be limitless opportunities to learn. I think this is why *The Pod Delusion* brings me so much joy. I feel like somehow my younger self would have been happy to grow up into the person I am now.

I guess getting to this point in my life has been the end result of a long line of serendipitous events—from having dual nationality, to meeting one of my best friends, Nicole, who then turned me to Twitter and from there I found James and *The Pod Delusion*. James was all the things I was—vegetarian, lefty and loved punk. We had both read the same essay by Bad Religion's singer Greg Graffin on being punk, which in turn shaped the way we thought of ourselves as punks. Being atheist and skeptics, this sort of coincidence isn't something we'd think was "meant to be" but it was surely serendipitous.

As Greg Graffin put it in the "Punk Manifesto": "PUNK is: the personal expression of uniqueness that comes from the experiences of growing up in touch with our human ability to reason and ask questions."

That's what *The Pod Delusion* lets us do. The world is ours to explore, interrogate and critically evaluate. We've made it our mission to broadcast what we think are "interesting things" to the world. Such a broad remit means that we can talk about everything from punk to science to politics, all in one show. We get to ask interesting people about interesting things, and the in the nature of the podcast be blown away by others contributing amazing stories all the time. For me, it is learning something new every week and remaining connected, interested and passionate about the good things in the world. It also means a lot of angst about the things that we find frustrating but that's what happens when you are interested in and passionate about the world around you.

We have laid claim to our small corner of the Internet and that might be all we ever do. However, it gives us the courage and motivation to interview people we never thought we would and go to events we never thought we'd go to. Along the way we get to meet people who have had us in their ears training for marathons, commuting or working in the lab.

We live in an extraordinary time where all this is possible (and almost commonplace) and in a country that doesn't censor us. It's hard to imagine how this could not bring joy into anyone's life. What gives it even more meaning for me, is that I get to do it with someone who shares my values, my ethics, my sense of social justice and also my ideal soundtrack.

HELENA GUZIK
ONLINE PUBLICATIONS ASSISTANT, THE METROPOLITAN MUSEUM OF ART
NEW YORK, NEW YORK

I love to hike but have never been fond of outdoor stairs. Something about a steep incline of harsh edges set into an otherwise lush landscape is unsettling. Needless to say, climbing the three hundred steps up to the Buddhist temple of Wat Phra That at the top of Doi Suthep during one of Thailand's brief but intense seasonal downpours was not the contemplative experience it might have been. Assessing my footing on the slick tiles consumed my mental energies; rather than concentrating on the literal ascent to enlightenment, I admit to being preoccupied with not clumsily plummeting back down to earth. My mood changed upon reaching the mountain's summit. Shedding my shoes, I wandered barefoot around the freshly rain-washed temple complex, dazzled by the glittering gold chedi (a Thai Buddhist reliquary structure); magnificent views of Chiang Mai and its environs opened up around this pinnacle of the landscape; and I was touched to discover the custom of leaving a written wish—a small part of yourself—attached to a little bell hanging in this communal space atop the mountain. I do not consider myself religious, but even so, my encounter with this site was transcendent. With or without faith, I was privileged to experience moments like this all over the world as I grew up.

My international background has certainly influenced my identity. I was lucky enough to divide my childhood between four different countries, on four different continents. I went to college and started my career in New York City (the world's capital!). In a few months I will move abroad again to pursue a graduate degree. A life of travel has shaped how I approach situations, relate to others, and find meaning in the world. Most importantly it instilled in me from a very young age the itch to explore, discover, and constantly learn. It is why I am drawn to academics and enjoy delving into questions about other peoples, places, and times. It is why I now have a job helping to make creative, educational resources accessible through digital media. It is why I still travel every chance I get.

The summer before my last year of college I visited Europe for the first time. The impetus for the trip was a grant for research in Italy, but my journey commenced with a study tour in northern Spain as part of a course on medieval pilgrimages—the Camino de Santiago in particular. For two weeks we woke at dawn, hiked through the countryside for 20–30 kilometers, then spent the afternoon exploring a new town and recuperating with other pilgrims. Though our class encountered the Camino from an academic perspective, the experience was naturally saturated with religion—it is, after all, a route that has been settled and traversed by devout Christians since the Middle Ages, as the innumerable churches, monuments, and relics will attest. Yet for all the faith-based rituals, each person seems to develop his or her own powerful relationship to the road, which is in no way diminished for nonbelievers. The sense of camaraderie that forms between strangers across national and linguistic divides, the awareness of your own body's capabilities and limits as you carry yourself and your belongings to each day's destination, the realization of just how small we all are in relation to our world when it takes a day and a great deal of effort to traverse the equivalent of less than an hour-long car ride—theists and atheists alike can appreciate these transformative elements of the Camino. My pilgrimage was not a religious one, but that does not mean it was any less valid.

When people ask where I am from, I cannot offer a simple answer—everywhere and nowhere both apply. I would like to think that globalization is pushing us all to identify more as world citizens than as members of distinct groups, segmented on the basis of religion, nationality, or tradition. Regardless of my stance on the divine and the afterlife, I will continue trying to make the most of my time in *this* world—eyes and mind wide open.

Buen Camino.

JAMILA BEY
JOURNALIST
WASHINGTON, D.C.

Each day I arise, I curse the alarm clock. I usually bicker with my child about what I'll let him eat for breakfast. And Hubby and I conduct our parallel dance of morning rush, brushing past one another and actually seeing one another with full intention only as we peck our daily goodbyes on the lips.

We mean to seize the day and to suck the marrow out of the bones of life, but somehow, it's hard to do with the kid gets jelly on your suit, or the crickets meant to feed the pet lizard manage to loose themselves from their cricket cage and pour into the living room.

And these moments mean that I am alive and that I am filled with gratitude.

I genuinely believe that there is no meaning to life. I am here by sheer accident of birth. There's no greater purpose, or deep and profound cause. My life, while sacred to me, is every bit as planned and predetermined as the life of the cow who died to become my burger.

Unlike poor Bessie, however, I choose to live my life each day in a manner that makes my life better, and improves the lives of my fellow human beings. I must create purpose and reason in my own life, and I get to have great fun doing so!

Spending time with family and friends, figuring out a new way to do a thing, or even just reading and debating with someone wiser than myself, each day presents a number of chances to connect with others or to come to better know myself in a meaningful way.

My life would be nothing if not for love, laughter and learning. There is absolutely nothing supernatural required. No professions of creed or allegiance needed, just the simple reward of being reminded that every breath and every experience is a chance to revel in the chance to savor being alive.

Of course, being human means too, that there are also great moments of sorrow. We can't escape the reality that there will be tears and pain, loss and sadness, and moments where we genuinely believe that we don't want to live on this planet anymore. Disappointment and betrayal are experiences as human as any other.

So why do it?

Greater minds than my own have tackled this question. Poets and philosophers have all come to conclusions about what makes this world and this existence one of purpose and substance.

And frankly, I love being able to say that I don't know what is the final answer. I don't know that I will continue to find meaning in the things that make me smile today. The joy though, in figuring it all out, brings me renewed delight with each opportunity.

Watching my child grow and discover the wonder and the greatness in the world has to me its own reward. Loving another and giving of oneself can be the greatest experience in a lifetime. Allowing oneself to be helped and pulled from a despair can illustrate that we are indeed all connected in some way.

I don't need gods or fairies to make me wonder. I only need to look at the world and the people I love therein and to know to myself, that it's not important as to why we're here. We each determine for ourselves. And that search gives me joy, gives me hope, and gives me meaning in my life.

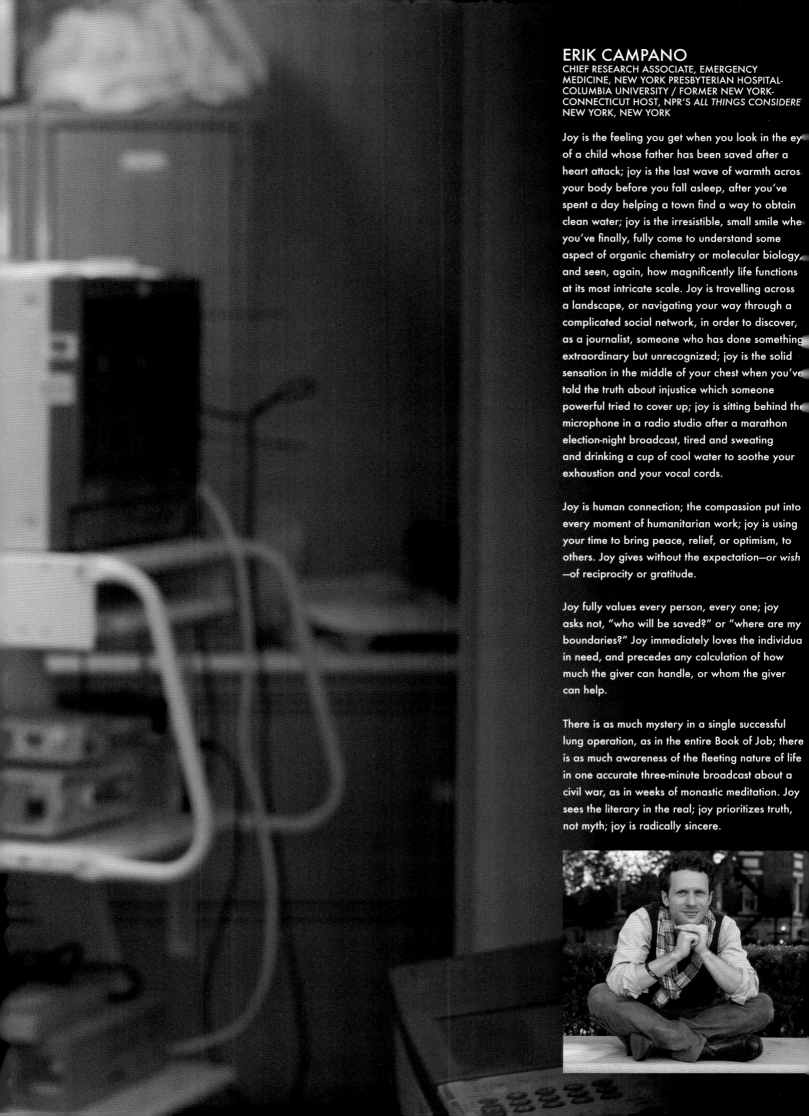

ERIK CAMPANO

CHIEF RESEARCH ASSOCIATE, EMERGENCY
MEDICINE, NEW YORK PRESBYTERIAN HOSPITAL-
COLUMBIA UNIVERSITY / FORMER NEW YORK-
CONNECTICUT HOST, NPR'S *ALL THINGS CONSIDERE*
NEW YORK, NEW YORK

Joy is the feeling you get when you look in the ey
of a child whose father has been saved after a
heart attack; joy is the last wave of warmth acros
your body before you fall asleep, after you've
spent a day helping a town find a way to obtain
clean water; joy is the irresistible, small smile whe
you've finally, fully come to understand some
aspect of organic chemistry or molecular biology,
and seen, again, how magnificently life functions
at its most intricate scale. Joy is travelling across
a landscape, or navigating your way through a
complicated social network, in order to discover,
as a journalist, someone who has done something
extraordinary but unrecognized; joy is the solid
sensation in the middle of your chest when you've
told the truth about injustice which someone
powerful tried to cover up; joy is sitting behind the
microphone in a radio studio after a marathon
election-night broadcast, tired and sweating
and drinking a cup of cool water to soothe your
exhaustion and your vocal cords.

Joy is human connection; the compassion put into
every moment of humanitarian work; joy is using
your time to bring peace, relief, or optimism, to
others. Joy gives without the expectation—*or wish*
—of reciprocity or gratitude.

Joy fully values every person, every one; joy
asks not, "who will be saved?" or "where are my
boundaries?" Joy immediately loves the individua
in need, and precedes any calculation of how
much the giver can handle, or whom the giver
can help.

There is as much mystery in a single successful
lung operation, as in the entire Book of Job; there
is as much awareness of the fleeting nature of life
in one accurate three-minute broadcast about a
civil war, as in weeks of monastic meditation. Joy
sees the literary in the real; joy prioritizes truth,
not myth; joy is radically sincere.

ROBERT LLEWELLYN
WRITER / TV PRESENTER / SPEAKER / ACTOR / ELECTRIC VEHICLE EVANGELIST
GLOUCESTERSHIRE, UNITED KINGDOM

[INTERVIEW] I'm blessed with the joy I get from successfully communicating with an audience. It's something I do regularly, and developing that skill over a long time has been hard work so I don't see it as a God-given blessing. When I started doing it I was shit at it, there's no other way of saying it. So it's something I've learned over many years, and to eventually find a forum where I can talk about something I'm passionate about and genuinely interested in, and to find an audience engaging with that, is rewarding beyond normal experience. I feel very privileged to have the opportunity to do that.

Then there's the struggle of family life, of being a parent. Witnessing your children's achievements is hugely rewarding, but it takes a while to sink in with me. Recently I went to my daughter's school where we met all her teachers, and they're really impressed with her. She's doing really well but I was quite stressed because I had to zoom off right afterwards to do a talk, so I was in a bit of a rush. Two days later when I had a moment to reflect, I realised they thought she was really good. I've somehow helped create this child who is full of questions and interest in knowledge, and reads avidly and wants to know who did what and when and how, which is immensely rewarding.

And my son, in a very different way, his artistic abilities are spectacular. When you see that in a child you've known so intimately since the minute they arrived on the planet, and now he's this big bloke. He could punch me out at whim but thankfully he doesn't. He has this beautiful ability and freedom to draw and capture things that spark his imagination, and I look at him and it's so extraordinary... it is a semi-religious experience. You know, how can he do that now, because he was so annoying and he'd eat crayons when he was a baby, he wouldn't draw with them. How does he develop into this amazing person? Where does that come from? It's an extraordinary thing to witness. So that certainly gives me joy.

Managing 25 years of marriage to one woman is incredibly fucking difficult, and at the same time immensely rewarding. It's not easy, but I'm really thrilled that we've both managed to do it. We may get divorced this evening, who knows, but we've done 25 years. I'm still with the missus, I'm absolutely thrilled. It gives me enormous joy to see her across a crowded room, and I go, God I love that woman, really a lot. How weird! I've known her so well, why don't I hate her like most of my mates hate their ex-wives? So many of my friends are divorced and I'm still with the same woman. Our combined history means that we have a kind of core of understanding with each other, and of joy with each other and of good memories. I have to keep reminding my family that we do have good memories because they quite like relishing the day when dad got cross that morning and threw the plate. Yes, one time!

The dawn chorus. I love that, and as I live in the country, it's very intense if you are awake early enough. But even if you wake up in the middle of London at, say, 4:30 in the morning on a summer's day, there's very little traffic noise. There is a dawn chorus in the middle of London, and it's a very loud period of about half an hour when all the birds just go ape-shit. They all sing, and it's just ecstatic, it's the most ecstatic sound. I've always loved it, it gives me enormous joy. There is the understanding, through science, why that happens, why they all sing at that time as the sun comes up, locating each other, how the world is spinning and how the sun is coming into view as you spin around. Even the cosmic level of it is based on effectively proven science rather than belief. And that fills me with joy rather than despair. I can understand why the sun doth rise. Of course, the sun's pretty much just staying still and we're going around it. I find that fascinating and bafflingly huge and enormous and humbling and also very fulfilling.

The more I've understood about how the universe works, the more awe has come and the more joy. Rather than going, oh it's just clockwork and it's not fulfilling in a spiritual way, the sun is there and we go around every year and all that stuff. No, I think that's amazing. It's extraordinary how that happens and how humans have slowly come to understand it, and how the human mind has been able to comprehend that, because it's much easier to just believe the world is flat and there's a man with a wheelbarrow with a bright light in it and he walks around a big staircase every day and he's called God. That's much simpler to understand. Actually, dammit, I think that might be true. I'm going to become a wheelbarrowarian.

MARLENE WINELL
HUMAN DEVELOPMENT CONSULTANT / AUTHOR
BERKELEY, CALIFORNIA

I feel content in water, especially salt water. My own body is mostly water and so is the surface of the Earth. I can blend and move with the current, and experience a sense of oneness. Since leaving Christianity, it has been a joy to let go of toxic ideas and try on other concepts, many of which were foreign and forbidden. A favorite one is the image of being a wave in the ocean—an idea from Buddhism. I can be an individual and yet part of a much larger whole.

I thrive on maintaining a simple awe about the universe. No matter what struggles we are going through the miracles of existence continue on, forming and reforming patterns like an unstoppable kaleidoscope.

Once, when contemplating these ideas lifted me out of a depressed state, I wondered about the source of my inspiration and did some musing, playfully giving it a personal voice:

Who is this from? This is from the force that makes the new shoot grow between concrete slabs. This is from the symmetry of fractals. This is from the incomprehensible distance of space. This is from the sound waves that blend and beat and tell you to dance. This is from the little child that looks at you clearly with no fear and says "Hi!"

This is from the unadulterated force of the sea under you and all around you when you swim in the ocean—the sea that takes no prisoners when the tide comes in, the sea that spawned life, and the same sea that sends a wave spreading up the sand to your bare feet, with rhythmic purring caress, bringing you the gems that make you smile.

This is from the cosmic red afterglow of the big bang. This is from all eleven dimensions of the multiverse. This is from all the things you don't understand and like that you don't understand. This is from the source feeding flashes of human greatness like the aquifer beneath all of you. This is from the power behind the form, the elusive explanation, the delectable mystery.

I have one thing to say and that is REMEMBER ME. You are not alone. You always have a reason to go on. Ineffable and inexorable, both. The tide is coming in again today. The ocean has not been pausing to decide about moving with the moon. You will birth another mystery...and another. Seed bursting, flower shooting, cracking concrete.

In my work I have the supreme privilege of working with amazing people I call "reclaimers"—folks who have left harmful, authoritarian religionsand are reclaiming their lives. I've learned so much and my clients inspire me. In addition, my awareness of religious mental and emotional child abuse motivates me to work to raise public awareness.

As a reclaimer myself, I find joy claiming my place in this world now, not in the hereafter. I'm here to dance, to love, to taste, to paint, to speak my mind—to live. As Amelia Earhart said, "I want to do it because I want to do it."

SEAN HUTCHINS

MUSIC PSYCHOLOGIST / POSTDOCTORAL FELLOW, ROTMAN RESEARCH INSTITUTE
TORONTO, ONTARIO, CANADA

What gives meaning to my life? Honestly, I think this is the wrong question. I don't think life has a meaning. Hell, I don't think life *needs* a meaning. Maybe it's just semantics, but the term meaning implies that there is an outside significance or a goal. For life to have meaning, it would have to have meaning to something else, and I (probably along with everyone else in this book) don't think that there is something else. So not only don't I think that there is some external meaning to my life, I don't think it needs to be given a meaning.

On the other hand, I have plenty in my life that gives me joy and brings me happiness—foremost among these are my children. My children and my wife. And an almost fanatical devotion to the Pope (are these edited?). *[Editor's note: Yes.]* Not to get overly schmaltzy, but there's something that will melt your heart when your kid tells you that they love you, or when you see them do something nice without being told to. Even just watching them develop from cute but mainly undifferentiated masses of baby to recognizable human beings is pretty cool.

My older son just asked me what religion was; he picked up the word from a book about Canada. I didn't really know what to tell him, partly because I don't really know myself. How do you explain the concept of an all-knowing sky-god to a kid who can't even figure out how to put on his pants straight? Especially while explaining it's not real? The kid thinks he can jump into a TV show, for chrissakes. My wife and I have talked about how to explain it to him. It's a fine edge to say there's something that a bunch of other people believe which we don't without sounding overly condescending.

Unlike many other atheists, I've never believed in god—I've never had a moment where I've "turned away" from the church. Sure, I was raised going to church, but it was a pretty liberal kind of church. We were taught to be kind and charitable, but the Jesus and angels thing always seemed optional, and there was a moment in maybe fourth or fifth grade where I realized that I didn't believe in all of that, and never really had. So I have no idea what it's like to believe in religion.

I used to argue about it with friends—rousing intellectual discussion among 16-year-olds and all that, but after a while, I realized that I was happier just not engaging with religion. There's an old Buddhist parable about an atheist who spends all his life thinking, "There is no god," and finds himself in heaven when he dies, because he kept god constantly on his mind. I think continually fighting against religion gives the idea strength. Not that there aren't battles to be fought, and wrongs to be righted, but the idea that it should be all-encompassing is not a path to a satisfying life (and this is the only one we get—a common theme here). I'm an a-theist, not an anti-theist, and the less a role in my life religion plays, the better. Life doesn't need a meaning, it just needs happiness. So if there's something I'd want for my children, it's not for them to push back against religion. It's for them not to have to worry about it at all.

Photo: Hutchins with his son Xavier

NICHOLAS ROBERTSON
COMMERCIAL AIRLINE PILOT
NEW YORK, NEW YORK

At the age of eight I boarded a large commercial jet bound for New York City to start a family vacation. It was the first flight of my life and I have had a passion for flying ever since. My love of flying quickly became obvious to those around me. I read about airplanes, doodled them, watched educational shows about them, and begged my parents to take me to the airport so I could watch them takeoff and land. My third grade elementary teacher told my mother that I would be an airline pilot. The dream job of every fifth grader was listed in our yearbook and my entry was of course "Airline Pilot." I did my book reports about airplanes and was even given aviation themed nicknames by my peers. My father worked to get his private pilot's license and took me flying with him multiple times in small propeller aircraft. Once he let me hold the control wheel as if I was flying even though my feet could not reach the rudder pedals, a fond memory nonetheless.

During my senior year of high school I began training to get my private pilot's license. The day I passed my FAA flight test and received my license will always be remembered with thrill and pride. I danced around the house the day I received my acceptance letter into Auburn University's flight education training program. My career path was taking shape. Collegiate flight training classes were challenging but I never lost sight of my ultimate goal, to fly professionally. Near the end of my last semester at Auburn I was hired by a regional airline to be a First Officer on fifty seat passenger jets. After graduation I was off to three months of airline training. During my first flight carrying paying passengers I remember thinking I could not believe that after fourteen years of dreaming about being an airline pilot I was finally there.

Flying is still such a rush even after twelve years in the cockpit. I cannot explain why I have always loved flying. The size, speed, and elegance of jets will always mystify me. Flight provides a tranquility when I am soaring several miles above the earth's surface observing its beauty below and the perfect distraction from life's stresses when I am fully concentrated on controlling the aircraft during a challenging takeoff or landing. I have never grown out of my passion for flying. This is the only life I am certain that I have so I find it necessary to enjoy it by spending my time with wonderful people and relishing in my favorite pastimes such as flying.

I have only identified as an atheist for the past few years, partly because there seems to be a negative connotation to the word in our culture today. When I was a child my family bounced from Baptist to Presbyterian to Unity and finally landed on the Church of Christ, but none of them ever made sense to me. My father was raised in the Church of Christ and my mother was the daughter of a Baptist preacher. I protested our church attendance but my mother told me I should be thankful because she had it much worse as a child and was forced to attend weekly services and the occasional weekend-long revival. It disturbed me that I was submitted to the same torture and boredom my parents seemed to loathe as children. Religion was an unwanted obligation that was performed strictly to appease my grandparents and fellow citizens in the community. I never enjoyed church and most of its teachings seemed illogical. Today I see religion as a tool used to take advantage of others for monetary and personal gain and as the driver of much hate in the world. I am proud to call myself an atheist and ecstatic with my decision to free myself from the poison and corruption in religion. The people in my life and life's experiences are what brings me happiness. I can say with certainty that I am the happiest I have ever been and simultaneously the farthest I have ever been from religion, which is not a coincidence. That gap only grows wider by the day.

NICA LALLI
WRITER / MUSEUM EDUCATOR / EDUCATION CONSULTANT
BROOKLYN, NEW YORK

I don't like being defined by what I am not. Atheist, non-believer, even my preferred moniker *nothing*, address what I am not. They fail to get at what I am.

I am a complicated person, as I think we all are. I have many ideas; some define me while others are passing fancies or fleeting passions. I have changed my mind, shifted my ideas, and developed my theories all my life. Thoughts, ideas, and memories meld with experiences to form more complex connections and directions. I can never say that one thing in the mélange of my brain is what defines me. I have many interests: cooking, nature, painting, baseball, teaching, watching cop shows on tv, knitting, sewing, and spending time with my family. I am a New Yorker, a Democrat, an oenophile, a foodie, a Yankees fan. I am also a heterosexual, an Italian American, a silver sister, an omnivore. I do many things—even in the course of one day I have many roles: mother, wife, educator, artist, writer, advice-giver, chauffer, dog owner, seamstress, cook.

The truth is that no one word or phrase says it all. Pick one. It will work—at least for a few minutes during my multifaceted day. But if you want to really know me, pull up a chair and let's really engage.

The problem is that no one really wants to get to know anyone else in a meaningful way. We don't have time. Sure, we know our small circle of friends and family, but anyone else has to fall into a category, quickly filed under some vague, non-specific term. Social media has only worsened this plight. We need to label people faster so we can group them, dismiss them, rally behind them, or despise them. Whatever...just make sure it is happening at lightning speed so we can get to the next page, screen, blog, or blip.

I don't really like labels. I think they keep us from actually getting to know one another. And let's face it, all the terms that describe people's beliefs are nothing more than labels. Once we determine someone "is" some religion—or no religion—we move on, thinking we know all about them. But what do we ever know from one word, whether it is Catholic, Protestant, Jewish, or atheist? We know nothing.

Perhaps that is why I favor *nothing* as a way to describe one part of myself. The fact that it is overtly meaningless is at least honest. And it makes people curious: "How can you be *nothing*? Don't you believe in anything?" To which I answer, "How much time do you have?"

JÖRG KLAUSEWITZ
NEUROPSYCHOLOGIST / PhD CANDIDATE
CONSTANCE (KONSTANZ), GERMANY

When I began studying clinical neuropsychology in Constance, I was overpowered by the beauty of the town as well as its surroundings. I was surprised that I was able to finish my study at a so-called elite "Excellence University," embedded in such breathtaking natural scenery. My partner Sabine and I wander in the mountains and spend a lot of time on the lake. The beauty of the mountains and the lake is completely evident without the existence of a Creator, however. One needs no God or another metaphysical authority to experience an emotional quality of the beauty of nature. I enjoy the rich fullness of its beauty. I don't feel the need to talk to a God in order to experience it. My own modest existence is moved in the right relation to this overpowering nature.

Working as a doctoral candidate in clinical neuropsychology allows me to ask questions which can lead to a radical understanding of ourselves and the world. This approach to generating knowledge from which others can profit fills me with great joy and passion. It's important to me that this knowledge is always under close scrutiny and is changed by new knowledge, or totally renewed by a paradigm shift. That is, science does not postulate the only truth, but questions itself over and over again.

I also see a central difference to religion, which provides in all its manifestations a central truth which is untouchable. This logically leads to the fact that their followers defend not only their views to the death, but have stopped asking questions.

However, interestingly this seems to apply only to certain areas of life. Most people—even religious—carry out an almost scientific investigation, for example, with something mundane like purchasing a car in order to receive the best vehicle for the best price. The same religious people, however, switch off this analytical thinking with substantially more important subjects which concern peacefully living together and continuity on this planet, counting instead on what is told to them Sunday morning in a sermon or written in a millennium-old book.

The landmark of the city of Constance symbolizes, in a satirical manner, this dualism of thinking and action at a political level. The 18-metre-high statue of the voluptuous courtesan Imperia commemorates the Council of Constance (1414–1418). Two naked little men sit in her hands. The man in her left palm wears the imperial crown of an emperor and holds an imperial orb; the figure in her right palm carries a papal tiara and sits with crossed legs. The two men represent worldly and ecclesiastical power or possibly even the emperor Sigismund and Pope Martin V.

To have the freedom to examine all statements carefully, to question everything and to be allowed to think about anything without restriction is a freedom which had to be won in the past, and must be defended over and over again in the future. To fulfill this freedom is what makes me a human being, and shows for me a sense of purpose in life.

Left: Klausewitz with his partner Sabine on the shores of Lake Constance

DERREN BROWN
ILLUSIONIST
LONDON, UNITED KINGDOM

[INTERVIEW] Where do I find my joy and meaning? I don't know if faith ever really gave me joy and meaning when I was religious, apart from hopping around at church. Perhaps a sense that I was OK and loved even if I felt low. People talk about where you find joy and meaning, and you're almost obliged to say now as an atheist, that you find your joy and meaning in science. But I don't know, it seems an odd thing to say. You may be joyfully disposed, or maybe you're not joyfully disposed, sort of fairly happy in a tranquil way. You might find that in a religious belief, or if you don't, you'll find it elsewhere, but either way, that comes down to your disposition. It's something that comes from you, it doesn't come from the thing you believe in. There's nothing inherent in Christianity or science or anything else that's particularly joyful or meaningful. It's just how you're disposed to interpret things. Personally, I find pleasure in reading, especially philosophy, in writing, in painting, in performing. As for meaning—I like the application of Nietzsche's idea of eternal recurrence—living your life in a way that you'd be happy to live it again and again. Beyond that, I don't know what meaning really amounts to. Living an examined life is, I think, important— but to create God as the embodiment of human meaning and then ask 'where is your meaning without him?' is a very weak, circular question put forward by some believers.

When I graduated and I was just about earning a living as a magician, I decided that I wanted to be able to take a cross-section of my life at any point, and think, 'Is this image of my life now, is that what I feel my life should be about?' And that's actually quite an easy thing to do, because it's not about ambition, it's just about thinking, 'Yeah, things are sort of arranged in the right way, and this is the life I'd like to be living'. And I've always had that, and as long as that feels like it's in place, that makes me happy. Sometimes the current snapshot might involve too much work, it might be too heavily work-geared and not enough pleasure-geared, and I try redress that if I can, so that my life feels like things are in balance, and I'm enjoying the things that I'm doing. That gives me an overall sense that things are right, and I also really like the tranquility of it. Far more worthwhile—and present-orientated—than having a series of ambitions. Obviously it's a process, not something that just suddenly happens, but if those things are in place, than I'm happy.

I tour every year, and that's hugely enjoyable. I really love that, and part of it comes from the fact I get my days free, so I can just sit and read and it gives me a lifestyle that's more in line with that ideal snapshot I try to have in place. If I have a bad day for any reason, the show clears that out with the adrenalin rush it provides. And we all need joys that transcend the everyday and make us feel bigger than ourselves. That's what religion can provide—Schopenhauer talks about religion infantilising the public as it provides a worthwhile truth but wrapped up in allegory, to provide a folk-metaphysics that everyone can swallow. But the priests and all involved have to pretend that it isn't allegory, that it's truth, for it to work. Of course you don't need pre-packaged religious 'folk-metaphysics' to have that transcendence in your life. I find it when I feel a general connectedness with people, when I suddenly feel warmth for all around me. The rush of warmth might come from an idea, or something I've just read or seen, taking root and changing my perceptions for the better, even if just for a few minutes. It's a lovely thing. And perhaps all the lovelier for not being immediately coloured by a lot of nonsense about some dodgy deity doing his work.

JESSICA AHLQUIST
STUDENT ACTIVIST
CRANSTON, RHODE ISLAND

[INTERVIEW] When I first got involved in the *Ahlquist v. Cranston* school prayer case, I wasn't doing it knowingly. It just kind of happened. And so people constantly ask me, "What inspired you to do this?" and I really don't know. I guess I was inspired by the law. I had seen this prayer banner and it bothered me. I've always been big on fairness and equality. That's what inspires me—equality, justness and fairness. So, when I saw this prayer banner I wanted to make it right and do the right thing. I never really set out to be an activist. Nothing ever inspired me to become involved in the atheist community and do this, but I had been inspired to do the right thing, and that's what led me into that battle—and this community.

It can be stressful to be put in such a spotlight, but things have quieted down since then. For a long time, the only attention I was getting was negative. It was people in the media or people on social networking sites calling me names and flinging insults at me or accusing me of seeking attention. Since then, it's become a lot more positive. A lot of conferences have invited me to speak and I've been invited to speak at schools. I have a lot more positive opportunities and I'm getting away from all of the negative stuff. I think it's definitely taken a better turn. I'm very thankful for that because it could still be terrible. I know that there are many people who are in the atheist community who still get death threats and I'm glad to say that I really don't anymore. I've definitely been lucky.

One of the coolest moments of my entire life was the day that I spoke at the Reason Rally in D.C. I had been in school all that week and people had been very hostile to me. It was a not a good time in my life. Then I went to the Reason Rally, and I was backstage in the tent because it was raining. I was waiting to go on, and terrified, but as soon as I got on stage...as soon as I was introduced, these 20,000 people below me just started cheering. They knew who I was and they supported what I was doing. That had to be one of the most uplifting feelings, because I had just come from a very hostile environment and had just driven eight hours and showed up at this place where everyone adored me. It was definitely the most supported I have ever felt.

They presented me with a scholarship that Hemant Mehta, *The Friendly Atheist,* had raised for me. It was proof that there are good people in the world, who support what I'm doing and it was amazing to see them all and feel that love.

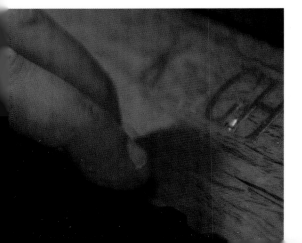

DAN BARKER
CO-PRESIDENT, FREEDOM FROM RELIGION FOUNDATION
MADISON, WISCONSIN

[INTERVIEW] I think meaning in life comes from finding a problem to work on and solving it. The problem can be different for different people, but you must find something that has to be done and determine how to do it. As a musician, creating songs that say what I want to say inspires me.

We have our thumbs, we're toolmakers. We have our brains, with reason. I think being engaged in a problem is what keeps us alive. It could be constructing something, or fighting disease. It could be political or social. It could be fighting hunger. It could be gaining knowledge or creating beauty.

When I was a preacher, much of my message was a denial of human nature, denial of who we are. We're all bad. We're all rotten. We're all sinners. We all deserve to go to hell. We all have to be under judgment, original sin, all of that, like there's something wrong with us. As an atheist, I don't buy into that paradigm anymore. Instead of original sin, I think about original good. Just being a natural human being with natural instincts, which are generally for good and helping others.

My greatest moments, though, are at the piano. I'll be playing this Saturday night at a restaurant here in town with a bassist, the two of us just jamming. We show up with no charts and no music. We just start playing and thinking and listening. It's organic. We don't even announce the key or the song. We have to figure it out and then right in the middle we'll change keys. It's just so much fun.

There are times when we're playing and we don't know if the audience is listening, but suddenly this magical thing happens where we're just sort of, "Whoa. Do you feel that?" And we look at each other and it's like an illusion. There's this big, capital "S," Song out there that transcends us. We know it doesn't, we know it's not really there. It's an illusion in our brains, but it's an illusion to live for. I think some religious experiences are like that.

One of my most important realizations was, and this might sound contradictory, the idea that in the big picture, nothing matters. We don't matter. Our lives, our struggles, our joys—all of that stuff in the cosmic picture doesn't matter. It's all going to disappear. It's going to be like an ant colony that got washed away with a flash flood. That's very liberating, because it means that what matters is right now. When the ants are doing their work and they're following their instincts, they're doing what they do, that matters to them now.

I used to preach that the good news was that Jesus died on the cross for our sins, so now we get to go to Heaven. But that's not the good news. The really good news is that there's no purpose of life. It seems contradictory. Everybody is asking, "What's the purpose of life? What's the meaning of life?" That's a theologically loaded question. If there's a purpose of life, that means there's something outside of life that gives us purpose. That means that we are secondary, we are subservient, or we're servants or members of some military or whatever. We're cogs in this machine above and beyond us, which actually diminishes our life. If there's a purpose of life, that actually cheapens life.

Elizabeth Cady Stanton spent a half a century fighting for women's rights. She didn't believe in some cosmic afterlife but she had a life of immense purpose trying to solve that problem. The concept that women should be equal participants in their own democracy was a big problem back then. She worked, fought and eventually she was successful. Margaret Sanger with birth control, Bertrand Russell with philosophy, Carl Sagan with science, and Johannes Brahms or Verdi with music, all these different fields where people are working, but not for some cosmic purpose. We have become the masters. We decide. We find the purpose and I think it's much more meaningful to find your own purpose within yourself than submitting to a Lord.

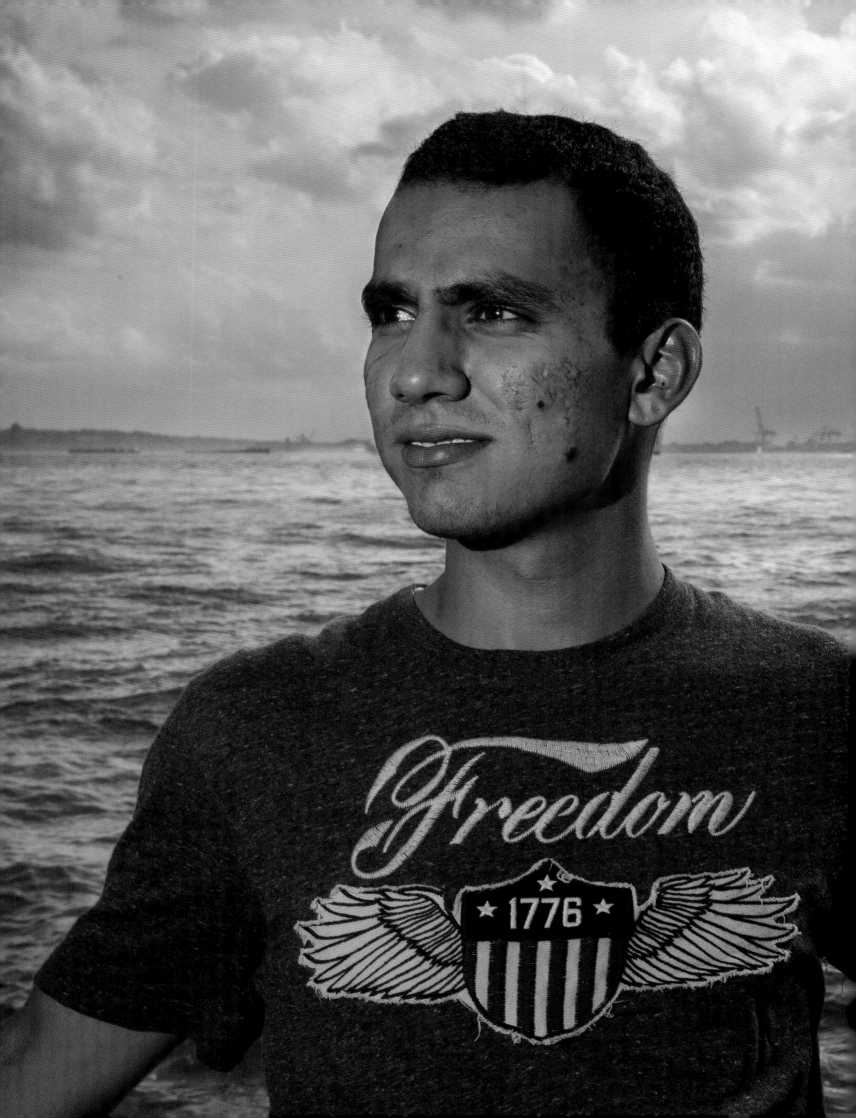

FAISAL SAEED AL-MUTAR
WRITER / ACTIVIST
WASHINGTON, D.C.

I believe all people are created equal. I am a firm believer in human rights and because of this I received my first death threat in 2007. I was still in high school. I was shocked to find bullets inside my back pack with a letter that said "You are next." That was the day my best friend was murdered a few meters outside of the school. As you can imagine, I was dismayed at the fact that within my own country I was being labeled and stricken with belittling, discrimination, hatred, and death threats to my person, ambitions, and dreams. The lack of respect for humanity in that society had never shown itself so deliberately until that time. In my desperation to maintain my sanity I clung to the dream of freedom. A dream that I could one day spread the message of peace and understanding to a society that would herald fairness. I wanted to be somewhere that I could expand upon ideas and principles that I knew to be true and fairly acquired by all of humankind upon birth.

One of the largest conflicts my society has faced is the right to religion, or lack thereof. So, after much research upon the U.S. Constitution, and its demand to create a life based on equality, I realized that the United States must be my new home—a place of safety, and of refuge.

I have left my home so that I may gain the courage and knowledge that the American revolutionaries had when they freed their people, and so that I may help spread the same message of purpose and privilege. I am not here to destroy the society I grew up in, as they may think, but only to be what I am, and that is a civilized human being. I hope to dissuade the cruel parts of the world from their self imposed exile, and persuade their audiences to understand that freedom is synonymous with life, and that the world is a place of safety and of refuge.

I am a simple man. I have no riches and do not desire them, but the power that I receive from books lets me know that we are all limitless and should always be so in our endeavors.

I realize there will be many obstacles, but I know that I will overcome them with an education and a lifetime of effort. I promise to work as hard as I can to take advantage of the opportunities that the brave souls of the past have created for me today.

So, now I ask you America, will you be my refuge, so that I can help make my potential exponential?

For life and liberty and the pursuit of happiness!

D.J. GROTHE
PRESIDENT, JAMES RANDI EDUCATIONAL FOUNDATION
LOS ANGELES, CALIFORNIA

[INTERVIEW] I think I'm happier than just about anybody else I know—so maybe there's a connection between my atheism and the happiness. Maybe it's just neurochemical, maybe it's my constitution, but when you think about meaning and the joy of life, you realize there are really sound and compelling reasons to be happy even if you don't live forever and in fact *especially* if you don't live forever. You value the three score years and ten you have on the planet all the more. What makes me happy now are relationships, and even if there's no God, you don't love your family any less. You don't love your children any less. You don't somehow stop caring about your parents or your spouse. So, what else? Work makes me happy, being productive, helping make the world a better place, all of that makes me happy and it's deeply gratifying. But I'd have to say that relationships are the most gratifying part of my life right now. And all of that is sort of Godless right? It's nonreligious but very robust and full and fleshed out and satisfying.

I do not believe that without God you can have ultimate meaning—so I agree with the Christian, the fundamentalist Christian, the evangelical who says if you don't believe in God you don't have ultimate meaning. I concede that point. I believe there is no ultimate meaning in the universe. But there's *proximate meaning*. There's meaning relative to human experience, to our lived experience. And I'm just fine with that. We decide our own meanings. There is no "thus sayeth." There's no top down meaning for all time and space and for everyone, but there's important and really meaty meaning for us in the limited time that we have here, and that's an important point that I think about a lot. You know, I'm almost 40 years old. I've been at this atheism racket for 15, 18 years and recognizing that you live in a Godless universe focuses your attention on your limited time and how precious it is and how important it is to make the most of every day, and not just for you in your little circle but for the planet. Indeed, when someone says without God there is no meaning—again, I'll concede the point that there's no ultimate meaning—but there's even

more proximate meaning. There's even more of an impetus or a prod to make the most out of your life right now. Evangelical Christians—I'm not trying to pick on those Evangelical Christians—but when you believe that your 70-plus years on the planet are essentially sort of meaningless because it's all something of a trial run for eternity, well that religious world view is in a sense, *nihilistic*. It makes our life meaningless. That retreat into the supernatural turns our back on what's most important: making the world a better place, our relationships, our loved ones, living the good life, the full good life. The extent to which you focus on the supernatural—as in Matthew 6:33 when Jesus says, "think ye on the things of the Kingdom of Heaven," and to make that your priority instead of the everyday workaday world—well, that is a denial of our human experience. *It's a rejection of the real meaning right in front of us.*

This sounds a little schmaltzy but I'm also inspired by my relationship with my partner. We've been together a long time, we're in our eighth year now, and it's inspiring to think of the plans and projects we have as we're building a life together and the fun and the play that we have. That's something we didn't talk about in terms of the good life, but the good life is playful. It's fun. There's laughing. There's a lot of boisterous, bouncy, happy fun in the good life we're talking about, and in that sense Thomas is inspiring because he is really one of the most playful people, he has more fun on that level than anybody I know. Now, he's also a super introverted person so most people who aren't close to us don't see that side of him, but it is inspirational. It's one of the great pleasures of my life to see that side of him on a day-in and day-out basis. Almost every morning he's sing-songy and cracking up, as we're getting ready in the morning, he's singing little songs. If I had a blank slate and I got the opportunity to redesign my life from scratch, that would be a component that I would not do without.

Photo: Grothe (right) with his partner Thomas Donnelly (left)

AYANNA WATSON

LAWYER / FOUNDER, BLACK ATHEISTS OF AMERICA
NEW YORK, NEW YORK

I love running. When I was younger, I use to race all of the neighborhood children. I was the fastest girl and able to beat a number of the neighborhood boys. I never considered running competitively as part of a team until junior high school. In seventh grade, I joined the varsity track team. My main events were the 400 and 200 meter relays. I remained on the team until my junior year of high school, when I decided to quit.

The next time I began running regularly was when I joined the military in undergrad. On average, we ran twenty miles a week over four days. The morning runs were one of the very few things I looked forward to during training. It was during these runs that I would forget that I was in military training and just enjoy being outside running. After I left training, I continued running for about a year and then I eventually stopped, as I had a difficult time finding room in my schedule to run.

In my second year of law school, my best friend had this crazy idea that we should run a half marathon together. I printed out a worksheet from a marathon training website and decided to take on the challenge. We completed the half marathon in October 2008.

No matter how long of a break I take, running has always provided feelings of relief and freedom.

Religion, on the other hand, was something that I always battled with. I felt like I was the only person who did not understand how to reconcile the obvious inconsistencies. The harder I studied, the more confused I became about religion. Like many, I did not know that not believing in deities was an option.

It was not until my first philosophy course in college that I began to question why I believed in the supernatural. By the end of the course, I was no longer a theist. It felt like a huge burden had been lifted off of my shoulders. Shortly thereafter, I began going to local atheist meetups and conventions.

Despite the fact that I met a number of awesome atheists, I could not help but realize there was a lack of diversity at the events. I began searching online for other atheists of color and learned that they too experienced a lack of diversity at their local events. These conversations online assured me that there was far more diversity among atheists than what is present at local meetups.

I decided that it was important to bring light to this diversity. I knew from my conversations online that many atheists were happy to meet other like-minded individuals but were disappointed in the lack of diversity. Whenever one of us was fortunate enough to meet another atheist of color, the feelings described were similar to what I experience every time I go running—feelings of relief and freedom.

I knew that if I could encourage more atheists of color to attend events, it would bring more atheists of color together. I chose to focus on the black American community, as it is the one that I grew up in. In 2010, I founded Black Atheists of America, an organization dedicated to bridging the gap between atheism and the black community.

ADAM PASCAL

MUSICIAN / ACTOR
LOS ANGELES, CALIFORNIA

"There's only us. There's only this. Forget regret or life is yours to miss" — Rent

[INTERVIEW] The hardest thing anyone can do is to truly love and accept oneself. We're all so concerned with achievement in life: attaining achievement, attaining material possessions, attaining a wife and children, whatever it is you want. We look to the future and the past, and we never experience the moments we're in. It's really difficult to do that, to truly experience the moments you're in, because you just want to get to the next moment. You feel like there's always something more down the road. And that line from *Rent*, really does speak to the understanding that life is finite. We have very few of these moments. We have very few days, and if you don't truly try to live in the moment and enjoy the moments that you have as you're living them, you'll never, ever be happy. If you're always looking to the next thing, then nothing will ever satisfy you.

You'll be on your deathbed and look back at your life, and realize you didn't enjoy those moments. There's nothing more to look forward to. It's over. And so I think that line from *Rent* was incredibly poignant, because Jonathan Larson, the writer of *Rent*, lived a very short life. I certainly hope he was able to believe those words himself and feel them—because if he was, he will have lived a much fuller, richer life at age 34 than most people live in lifetimes three times that long. That's something that is so difficult for us to achieve, to live in the moment and enjoy the moments as they happen.

We are all given a gift of existence and of being sentient beings, and I think true happiness lies in love and compassion. I've been thinking a lot about Zen Buddhist practices, and what I find so interesting about their teachings are how you learn to be a good person by looking inward. By becoming a happy person yourself, you are able to absorb happiness from around you and cause other people to be happy. The act of compassion is the main focus of those teachings. Most religions don't tell you how to be happy, they just tell you how to act. They give you a set of rules and say, "Follow these rules. This is how you're supposed to behave." But that doesn't help a person live a happy life.

I find it really enlightening to explore these methods of making oneself happy through love and compassion and inner peace. That is something I've struggled with my whole life. It's hard to be a human being. It's hard to live. Our brains are wired in such a way that our egos and our desires and wants are constantly fighting against spiritual growth. To find that balance, I think, is what I'm after.

Photos: Pascal in his dressing room, preparing for the musical Chicago

ANNIE LAURIE GAYLOR

CO-FOUNDER, FREEDOM FROM RELIGION FOUNDATION
MADISON, WISCONSIN

[INTERVIEW] I enjoy baking. I just brought in a Bundt cake and we have a game to guess the secret ingredient. (We do a lot of eating around the office!)

As for the purpose of life, it's what you make it. There wasn't a deity that put me on earth and said, you're going to enjoy baking, or you need to start a group to get God out of government.

Working for the First Amendment gives you profound meaning; I can't really think of anything more important. Certainly there are some things just as important, but it's right up there. And what gives you profound meaning is that you can make a difference, you can see the pendulum swing back. It's profoundly meaningful to start a group with two people and watch it grow to 19,000—the nation's largest association of atheists and agnostics—and to look back and see what we've accomplished and to have so many ambitions to do more.

What I'm really interested in is undoing the many First Amendment violations that occurred around the time I was born. The 1950s were a very problematic time for our secular Constitution. It's

kind of ironic that I've spent my life trying to undo some of these things that happened back then, such as "under God" in the Pledge of Allegiance in 1954, "In God We Trust" as a motto on our money, the National Day of Prayer that was enacted in 1952. I'd like to restore respect for the separation between state and church, and that gives a great deal of purpose to my life.

But personally of course, I'm just like everybody: You find your niches, you find what gives you pleasure. A lot of that is helping other people or doing things for other people. For instance, I work with The Women's Medical Fund, the abortion rights charity that my mother, Anne Gaylor, co-founded and still runs at age 86. It was created by atheists and today is the longest-lived abortion rights charity in the country, having helped more than 20,000 women throughout its history. There's a myth that atheists don't start charities. They certainly do. I think her lack of religion was really one of the reasons why my mother was able to start and run that charity. It wasn't something that would come out of religion at all.

Lots of things inspire me, my mother of course chief among them. Historical figures who made

changes, people like Margaret Sanger and Elizabeth Cady Stanton. And I'm also inspired by many of the people I work with who are part of the free-thought movement, or are taking lawsuits. People like Jessica Ahlquist or Jim McCollum, whose mother took a lawsuit that has done more to keep religion out of schools than any other Supreme Court case. I've had the opportunity to meet and work with so many Supreme Court litigants and it's very inspiring. Even an everyday member who joins our "out of the closet" billboard campaign, which takes a lot of gumption, or parents who stand up for their children's rights by complaining about religion in school. I think they're all very inspirational.

HOUZAN MAHMOUD
ACTIVIST / GRADUATE STUDENT, UNIVERSITY OF LONDON
LONDON, UNITED KINGDOM

I celebrated my 40th birthday, and actually it was the first time I ever celebrated a birthday. It was not a simple occasion; I invited almost 50 people—men, women, and children who number among my dearest and closest friends. I chose a great place—a venue in London, on the second floor of a Cypriot/Turkish restaurant—where we could be free to dance, drink and socialise until late at night. My only daughter's presence (she was 13 at the time) made this occasion extra special to me. Here I was among my wonderful friends, great food, music, wine, conversations, and dancing. At my 40th birthday celebration, seeing my daughter beside me, happy and enjoying herself, meant the whole world to me.

Celebrating my 40th birthday was just a crazy idea. I felt different, I felt free, I felt special, and I wanted to share my happiness with my friends who have always supported me in my political work. My life has always been about politics since I grew up in Kurdistan in Iraq, where we had to endure dictatorship and ethnic cleansing, meaning no freedom, no joy, no birthday celebrations, and no sense of normality. My family was involved in armed struggle for over a decade against the Ba'athist regime, a regime which people in the West consider to be "secular" although in fact our society was still haunted by religious superstitions, mosques, and traditions which were anti-women and anti-freedom in general. We were taught and brought up in a culture in which Islam had deep roots and dictated every part of our lives. The

ideas of guilt, shame, filth, and fear were part and parcel of our upbringing, both in schools and at home. Being female was not easy: control and limitation over our movements and way of life was always in place. The entire society was structured in a way that made it impossible to live your life according to your own will. I had never celebrated my birthday in my country, and the only joy I had was the joy of the political resistance despite its dangers.

Routine and normal life were distant dreams for my family. Our involvement in politics changed our perspective on life. Danger of being imprisoned by the regime, always hiding, being separated from my siblings every now and then, and spending a big part of my life in this way gave a different taste and a different idea of what life is. I should admit that this way of life taught me a lot. Being part of a political family was not a choice but a fact, and I have always been proud of my past and my family's history of struggling for freedom. I was lucky, though, in that my brothers, who were Marxists, helped me in realising my position in society as a female and realising especially how religion enforces suppression of women.

Growing up in a conservative society as a female was not easy for me. However, when I decided to celebrate my 40th birthday and look back at my past years and what I have gone through, I also got a chance to look back at so many

achievements in terms of my own freedom, and the struggle for rights and dignity for my people.

One of the most amazing achievements of my life is the power to free myself from religious superstition, starting from when I was 18. I have nothing against people who have religions, but for me living in a culturally and religiously restricted society was a big deal. Islam meant growing up in fear and feeling guilty all the time. There was something wired about this feeling and it was all to do with our sexuality as females. I felt that being a Muslim woman and living my life according to the words of a prophet who lived 1,400 years ago was really difficult. At the same time, my thinking, ideals, and perspective on life would have been so limited and framed. When I decided to leave Islam I felt relieved, like a bird in the sky, flying freely for the first time without thinking of being guilty, without the fear of Heaven and Hell.

Being an atheist gives me the feeling that I live my life according to my own will, and I am not scared. I have no fear in my heart and I enjoy my life. After all, when you tell yourself there is no Heaven or Hell, and why should I not enjoy this life, it is a big achievement in itself. So I am happy to have celebrated my birthday for the first time and on such a big scale; I truly enjoyed my birthday party in the presence of my wonderful daughter and friends.

CAMERON THORNBERRY

GRADUATE STUDENT / STUDENT NAVAL AVIATOR
CAMBRIDGE, MASSACHUSETTS

I love life, plain and simple. As a relatively young person, I anticipate a whole life to be lived, personal relationships that wait to be kindled, and countless milestones that ache to be achieved. I consider myself a very positive, passionate, and outgoing person, and in all honesty I've harbored few doubts about my path in life. I credit my outlook to one simple understanding that we all must individually confront: I will die. Maybe not today, maybe not tomorrow, but someday, I will die. Our life is governed by a finite number of heartbeats, and at first that is a damn chilling thought.

As macabre as the topic of death may sound, I've actually thought about it from an early age. In contrast to the many apostates who become atheists, my path to atheism and my ensuing optimism came early and did not include an initial passage through a traditional religion, even as I explored the potentially depressing and sobering concept of death. I think it is often this fearful and somber consideration of death that drives human beings to believe that there is a rosier state of being on "the other side." Supernatural assuages aside, I challenge with my own reflections the often grim assumptions and apprehensions that we as a society hold regarding death. Although I cannot trace it back to any one particular event

growing up, as I prodded further in my personal thought experiment of death, it was as if a veil was suddenly lifted and I experienced serenity and found ultimate meaning in *my* life.

I came to understand that I have been given a solitary shot at my life's underlying trajectory, and that the earlier I am able to figure out what I *truly* want to do with my life, the better that path will be. For me, this understanding has spawned a lifelong love of learning and propelled into reality my childhood dream to become a military pilot. (In full disclosure, although close, I am not completely there!) Regardless, this understanding has helped me spurn excuses to live a vanilla life and instead live fully whenever and wherever possible. As a result I've felt the exhilaration of getting lost on foreign shores and meeting complete cultural strangers, skydiving solo from 13,000 feet, moshing in the centers of metalcore concerts, and busting my ass in long-distance triathlons. The inevitability of death fundamentally fuels the thrill of these challenges I hold so dear, and I want—nay—I *need* to get outside and charge ahead until I have nothing left to expend; I don't want to die afraid or with remaining excuses.

Our bittersweet contract with death adds tremendous value and weight not only to my

life, but to the lives of those around me and to those I have yet to meet or will never meet. I sincerely do my best to enjoy and appreciate the time I'm able to spend with others, especially loved ones, because I never know for sure if this shared moment right now might be our last time together. It is death and the understanding of impermanence that makes me want to hug just a little harder when we say goodbye, knowing the potential exists that it might be our last. It is death that makes me want to smile at and connect with complete strangers on the street. And it really is death that propels me, out of love and respect, to want to better this world for future generations. Although our culture tends to ignore the topic of death and dying, I know its stinging reality can bite unexpectedly. Because of this essential understanding, my ultimate purpose and meaning in life is to fully embrace each day with open arms and share my love with those around me as long as I have the opportunity.

Carpe diem.

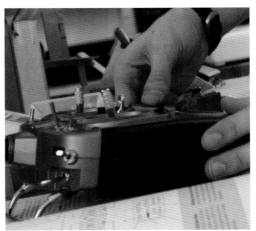

SEAN FAIRCLOTH
AUTHOR / FORMER STATE LEGISLATOR AND MAJORITY WHIP / LAWYER / LOBBYIST
WASHINGTON, D.C.

[INTERVIEW] You've got a very limited amount of time. Say you live to 90, say you live to be 100. It's a pittance. It is so minimal in the context of the history of this planet, that all you really have is this beautifully precious commodity, and that's minutes—and each minute you can decide what you do with that time.

And for me, the most beautiful thing you can do is make the world better. I'm not Van Gogh (unfortunately for me). I'm not a brilliant film director, so I think to myself, what can I do that makes the world better? I feel some sense of confidence and satisfaction that I can engage in social change where you can actually achieve a positive result. And so for me, that's where the greatest joy and satisfaction is: did you make the world better and can you pass that on to children, to the next generation?

You're like this little blip of light that lasts for a very brief time and you can shine as brightly as you choose. Religion can become an excuse to say, "Well I'm going to put that off...I'm going to ask for forgiveness later...Things are going to be great in the next world." For me, it is right now. Are you going to help in some substantive way in making this world a better place now? And if you are, then to me, that is the brightest light that you can shine. So I'm very skeptical about the idea that there is something special or valuable about deferring that to some imagined future period.

I started a children's museum back home in Maine. It really did something positive for young people. I introduced laws when I was in politics (for ten years) that I thought could help others, and I got over 30 of those laws passed. And that involved working with a huge variety of people. So for me, that is the greatest beauty—when you work with a team of people, get results, and say, "The world is better now!" and you have that sense of accomplishment.

I know a lot of people have had that similar experience where you've worked on something for a period of time, and you really think your accomplishment will last in a beautiful and meaningful way among us humans. So, as beautiful as I think the stars are (and I like the stars, I like the mountains), what I like most is people. To see people accomplishing something together—that is the greatest meaning for me.

I'm sometimes shocked at how lucky I am because when I write in my book about social change, related to reason and science, I actually am lucky enough to be in a position where I have huge opportunities and indeed leverage to effectuate some of that change. So, it's not just an abstract idea in my book. I'm able to use my political experience and background to articulate how we can effectuate that change.

I feel that in our society now, even though everybody talks through Facebook (which I like) or through Twitter (which I also like), I really value going to people and connecting directly, and using those connections to do things that are transformational and positive.

Within humanism, or secularism, atheism, etc., there is a disdain for the emotional, a disdain for appeals to people's heartstrings. That's wrong. That's logically wrong. If you are logical about the goal, if you want to change mass society, change the way a culture works, if you want to shift to a society based on reason and science—then, to achieve the ultimate goal, you in fact have to use an emotional appeal to open that doorway.

If I can bring you in with an anecdote, with this emotional story and it opens that door for you, then maybe you will go to the next step and say, what is the reasoning behind that? We can get people to use reason. That's where humanity has been headed at an accelerating pace since the enlightenment, over the past 400 years or so.

When you look at the history of our species, only for a few hundred years have we really systematized the use the scientific method in a rigorous fashion. This can really be beneficial to our fellow humans. That's what we can accomplish, and interestingly, and paradoxically we can use emotion to bring people into that worldview.

ANNA BELLA CHAPMAN
WRITER / ACTRESS
NEW YORK, NEW YORK

I grew up with a Brazilian Catholic mother and a staunchly rational English father. As you can imagine, there were countless family intellectual debates as to what my upbringing would hold spiritually. In the end, it was decided that I'd have the opportunity to sample both sides of the coin.

I was quickly rushed off to be baptized (I was eleven, and it was a peculiar experience to say the least), and then, after the requisite Sunday school, I was confirmed. Atheism was a decision that was mine to make and that meant something to me, as well. It's a choice I think upon daily. Having been exposed to both, I can say that the only appeal for me about religion was the ritual, the comfort that it brings. And so, in my late teens, I decided that those "blessings" should not be limited to those only with "faith."

Reading was always an escape, an adventure, a form of worship. Hell, maybe if the bible had been penned by Kurt Vonnegut I wouldn't be writing this now. I was not a "joiner" as a child, being painfully anxious and shy socially, so reading was a huge outlet for me, a world of friends and adventures that would not abandon me if I laughed at the wrong moment or wore the wrong thing.

The heroines whom I read about had no concept of right and wrong beyond that which they formed for themselves or learned through interaction with others. Morality is innate—an instinct to better ourselves, to help others, not to attain peace in a fictitious afterlife for our own benefit—but to enrich our lives here on earth, now.

Now to apply that to real life...terrifying. Where could I meet these like-minded fighters of evil? If not church, what meeting ground did I have? This is where my generation lucked out. We have the Internet for these kinds of things! Not only can I tell the world how I feel about it, but so can you, and so can the people who disagree with me! I began to look online for places I could excel: I took a sword class, I signed up for a bread-baking course, I even started a pen pal–type book club with a few kids in Japan.

And when I feel the need to commune with a higher power? I'll grab my old worn copy of *Still Life with Woodpecker* and go to Central Park with my camera. Or I'll drink a cup of tea, go to the Metropolitan Museum of Art, or have coffee with a peer I find inspiring and interesting. The world is all around us, (*here* and *now*), and it has so much more to offer than some of us were led to believe. My joy comes from myself and from the beautiful creatures I interact with everyday...even the religious ones.

Above: Anna Bella Chapman with her father Matthew Chapman
Below: Matthew's great-great grandfather Charles Darwin

MATTHEW CHAPMAN
WRITER / DIRECTOR / JOURNALIST
NEW YORK, NEW YORK

All an atheist loses by not believing in gods is a shortcut to an illusion. Every real pleasure remains, heightened by knowing life is finite. Here is one of a thousand alphabets I could have come up with of things that make life worth living. **Art.** More illuminating (and fun) than all religious texts on earth. **Brain.** I was going to say Breasts because they offer the first pleasure and generously continue to please even after their job is strictly speaking done. But a brain can imagine a breast, while the reverse is not true. **Coffee,** the most delicious stimulant on earth, reason enough to wake up. **Dreams.** Surreal elusive partners. **Empathy.** Children have it before religion can lay claim to it, it changes sorrow to solidarity, and makes pain bearable. **Friends.** The opening of a door, a sudden laugh, an embrace. **Grace:** in defiance, in loyalty, and in dying. **Hitchens,** Christopher. He had a rich life, sought knowledge everywhere, enjoyed the swiftness of his brain, a good fight, and a drink now and then. **Irreverence.** The witty expression of a brave free mind. **Jell-O.** Cold and slippery and refreshing. **Kids,** epic love, epic adventure, and K, my mother's best friend, a beautiful woman, aide memoire. **Literature** saved my life when I was fifteen and the world made no sense. **Movies.** Despite the decline of American movies into the endlessly recycled spectacle of bullies beating their chests and dubiously protesting "I *am* a Superhero!"—some artists don't succumb, and the library remains largely intact. **Natural Selection.** So self-evidently obvious and simple (once someone had the idea) you can explain it to a child in under a minute. **Orgasm.** Some living things procreate without having sex (call that living?) but not us! Nature *akbar!* **Partnership.** The gratification of creating something with other people. **Questioning.** A pleasure limited by faith, an infinite joy to the free mind. **Reading.** To drink at the deepest reservoir on earth. A smart reader becomes immune to propaganda; is capable of expression; is part of a great ecosystem of wisdom; and need never be bored. Reading is the way and the truth and the life. No one comes to enlightenment except through reading. **Swimming** in the ocean makes me feel awash on the globe, connected to everything. I am also reminded, as with bike riding, of the first ecstatic moment of learning how to do it. **Travel** makes me a child again. Everything is new and different, and yet—astonishingly—you realize that everyone wants almost *exactly* the same things out of life as you do and that the small but lethal differences are a creation of tribalism and religion. **Universe.** I look upward on a clear night, try to begin to apprehend the enormity of it, and am comforted by my insignificance. **Variety.** There are so many different people, places, foods, colors, emotions, arts, etc., *ad infinitum*. Five senses, billions of experiences. What luck. **Work.** I did ten years of largely manual labor before I was 25. Sometimes it was hard (I was a bricklayer in winter, for example), but we were in the same boat. It kept me sane then and keeps me sane now. **X-Rays,** along with vaccination, have saved billions of lives. In fact, I probably wouldn't be writing this and you wouldn't be reading it were it not for one or both. **Yellow.** Sand, the blazing sun, bananas, polenta, sometimes the moon. **Zebras.** I hope I see one in the wild before I die.

TODD B. SMITH
ENGINEER
PEORIA, ILLINOIS

In 1996 I got the opportunity to work in Grenoble, France for three years. I was 32 years old at the time, and up until then I had not traveled much—certainly nothing outside of the United States.

Grenoble is a city nestled in a Y-shaped valley between three different mountain ranges. As a Midwesterner, I was fascinated by the mountains. That fascination manifested itself in a strong desire to hike them, which I did many times. My feeling of exhilaration upon reaching a summit is still fresh in my mind, 15 years later. My first summit gave me a feeling of conquest, but after several more hikes that feeling slowly gave way to one of serenity and introspection. My perspective on the world was different when viewed from the top of a mountain. I could see the grandest features of the landscape all around me, yet still focus on a wisp of smoke lazily drifting out of a chimney from a house in the valley 2000 meters below. Those times when I experienced the combination of both the great and the small were some of the most joyful moments in my life.

I've come to terms with how small my life is relative to the whole universe. That feeling has made me appreciate the small things, the simple pleasures, all the more: the unbridled joy of my niece and nephew as they play with my dog Maggie, seeing the flash of insight in someone else's eyes as they learn something new, sharing a knowing glance with the one I love.

When I returned to the States, I brought back with me a new sense of wanderlust that is as strong now as it ever was. I've traveled to many other countries since my stint in France, and in each I have found diverse politics, values, and religious beliefs. I've learned that each of us is responsible for finding joy and meaning in our lives. As different as we all are, the one thing we have in common is perhaps the most important: a shared humanity. I'm awestruck when I imagine the grandness of humanity that populates the planet and the potential for each of us to lead fulfilling lives. But I suspect the same thing is true for each of us: it is the small things that bring us joy. And that is the grandest thing of all.

JAMES RANDI
MAGICIAN / FOUNDER, JAMES RANDI EDUCATIONAL FOUNDATION
FORT LAUDERDALE, FLORIDA

[INTERVIEW] I was a peculiar kid in many ways. I admit that freely. For one thing I was a "child prodigy," which was sort of unheard of in my neighborhood and was looked upon as some terrible disease or other, an affliction, certainly. I was allowed to skip school and was actually given a small card that I could have in my pocket. It was beige in color. I kept it in my pocket—I didn't have a wallet in those days. It was to show to any truant officer who might find me out of school. I was privileged not to have to go to grade school, generally speaking. I went when I wanted to and I went when the examinations, the tests, were held at regular periods. Otherwise, I was free to wander around.

I thus mixed with much older folks, certainly older children, high school and college kids in many cases. But it was an unhappy time for me. I thought it would be, "Oh that's fun. I can be out of school. I can go down to the Casino Theater on Queen Street." That was a variety theater that featured film and variety acts and that was almost my undoing in the long run, because up until then I felt that I wanted to be an archeologist or an astronomer, perhaps even an organic chemist, jobs which rather fascinated me.

Then one day I fell into the snare and never got out of it: I saw Harry Blackstone Sr. He was the reigning magician of the day and he'd come to the Casino Theater at least once every year for a couple of weeks. I went in and I paid the money for the matinee, sat in the first balcony, and saw Harry Blackstone levitate a woman in the air! Now the other magic tricks that he also did were wonderful, fascinating, entertaining, amusing, but the levitation of Princess Asrah, how could you possibly explain something like that? He had a lisp, did Harry Blackstone Sr. (I got to know Jr. many years later in New York City.) Harry stood there and said, "Asrah, rise!" and the young lady in the beautiful shimmering gown on a couch slowly rose into the air. He caused her to rise until she was up just above his eye level, and there

he stopped her. The band stopped playing and he stepped forward. He said, in his lispy way, "Ladies and gentlemen, you see this young lady suspended in the air between Heaven and Earth, so to speak. Should I so desire, she would stay there forever, but in the interests of time and of your patience, I will once again cause her to return to the couch from which she rose only a moment ago. Watch. Asrah, descend!" The music started up again. She very slowly came down to the little couch. He helped her to her feet, she stepped forward and took a bow, and I almost fell out of the balcony. I was totally fascinated. I had to learn what this was all about. I thought, that's not "magic," I'm sure. It's an illusion of some kind, but I've got to know. So I went backstage. The show was over and I actually walked out of the theater and around to the alleyway at the back and I saw old man Blackstone with his wing collar open, dressed in tails. There was no air conditioning in theaters in those days, remember. I walked over to him very boldly—at the age of 12—and introduced myself. He put his arm around me and took me back into the theater and I walked through all of the equipment. I didn't understand a bit of it, of course.

He showed me how to do a simple trick and then he gave me a poster, a very famous poster nowadays. It's very rare and it fetches huge money in the poster market. It was one of Blackstone levitating a camel. I don't know if he ever did that trick on stage, but he was shown levitating a camel, with his hands up in the air. He signed it for me, to "Randall," which is my original first name. He rolled it up, put a bit of string around it, and gave it to me. I tucked it under my arm, left the theater. I'm sure I was high above the ground as I left the theater. I went to the streetcar, took the streetcar, transferred over to a bus, and went home realizing that it was getting dark outside and my parents were probably in a terrible panic, which they were. I finally got home, ran up the front walk, burst into the door and my mother said, "Where have you been? We were

going to call the police!" I said, "I went to see Harry Blackstone at the Casino Theater and he showed me a wonderful trick. I can show you in a minute but he gave me a poster..." Uh-oh... I had left it on the bus.

Somewhere in Toronto, Canada, there may still be a bus which in the back window has a rolled-up poster from Harry Blackstone saying, "to Randall." If anyone would care to look in the back of every bus they go into... It was a long time ago. Maybe they've cleaned the bus since. I'm not sure. I lost that poster, but somewhere in the universe I think there still exists a levitating camel poster with my name on it and it belongs to me. So there!

There's nothing more exciting for me than looking into the eyes of a very young baby, someone three or four months old of either gender of course, any variety, any color, size, or shape, and just wondering, "What is going to become of you, little one?" What a wonderful inquiry. I know I won't get an answer to it but the potential is there. This is a human being in a formative state, going to be subject to most of the things that we're subject to in our lives, and what is going to become of this child? Will he or she become a doctor or a lawyer? Or even a politician; what a dreadful fate, in my estimation! A scientist perhaps? I mean, there are endless possibilities depending on the family's means, of course, and the vicissitudes of fate. We're all subject to that, and we may even get struck by a meteor or an asteroid. That's very, very, highly unlikely, but we can also be struck by a grand idea somewhere along the line that will set us thinking and make us wonder. As soon as we begin to wonder we begin to grow and children that age are just on the edge of starting to make those discoveries. I find that very exciting, very exciting, just looking into the eyes of a baby like that and I say, "Bonne chance," good luck. I hope you do well.

William M. Briggs

THE ARCHIMEDES PALIMPSEST PUBLICATIONS

THE
ARCHIMEDES
PALIMPSEST

VOLUME II
IMAGES AND TRANSCRIPTIONS

EDITED BY
Reviel Netz, William N
Natalie Tchernetska, and N

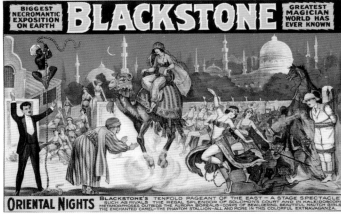

BIGGEST
NECROMANTIC
EXPOSITION
ON EARTH
BLACKSTONE
GREATEST
MAGICIAN
WORLD HAS
EVER KNOWN

ORIENTAL NIGHTS
BLACKSTONE'S TENFOLD PAGEANT OF THE EAST – A STAGE SPECTACLE
SUCH AS RIVALS THE REGAL SPLENDOR OF SOLOMON'S COURT AND IN KALEIDOSCOPIC
METAMORPHOSES OUTBIDS THE AURORA BOREALIS—CORPS OF BEWILDERING, BEAUTIFUL NAUTCH GIRLS
THE ENCHANTED CAMEL–THE PHANTOM STALLION–ALL AND MORE IN THIS COLORFUL EXTRAVAGANZA.

GAD SAAD

PROFESSOR OF MARKETING, CONCORDIA UNIVERSITY
MONTREAL, QUEBEC, CANADA

I am a Lebanese Jew by heritage and an atheist by conviction. Growing up in the Middle East, I quickly learned that daily life was experienced via the prism of one's religion. Yet, from my earliest memories of attending the Maghen Abraham synagogue in Beirut, I felt detached from the requisite religious rituals that shape communal living in the tribal societies of Lebanon. My inborn disdain for religion was further exacerbated by our having to escape the Lebanese civil war under the imminent threat of execution, which led to our family's emigration to Canada. On one of their return trips to Lebanon, my parents were kidnapped by Fatah to eventually be rescued after several deeply harrowing days of captivity. A constant reminder of the deep hatred that religion engenders toward out-group members thus shaped my childhood.

It is an affront to human dignity to suggest that purpose and meaning in one's life can only be garnered via the belief in a deity. To lead a rich and righteous life is more laudable when pursued void of the "guiding" edicts of a dictatorial higher power. My life is fulfilling in endless earthly ways be it via my intellectual and scientific pursuits; my university teaching; the love that I share with my family members, beloved canine companions, and close friends; traveling to new lands to immerse myself in new cultures and awe-inspiring landscapes; nourishing my being with knowledge, music, art, and films; and innumerable other daily quests, each of which reminds me of the magic of life.

Carpe diem (seize the day) is best instantiated when one recognizes the ephemeral and finite nature of our existence. There are no supernatural do-overs or eternal afterlives. My lack of religiosity makes it easier for me to appreciate the importance of every second, every minute, and every hour. You get one shot to experience life fully and hopefully make a difference. To assuage the existential angst inherent to our ever-looming mortality, I say: Fear not, immortality can be achieved but not via a religious-based afterlife. As a loving father to my children, I am effectively propagating my genes while as an author and professor I am disseminating my memes onto future generations. To recognize the evolutionary roots of our lifelong pursuits does not render them any less awe-inspiring. Instead, science and reason liberates us from the shackles of superstition by offering us a framework for understanding our shared humanity. Ultimately, we all have the capacity to treasure life and enrich the world in incalculable ways, none of which require adherence to religious dogma.

Having experienced the horrors of religious-based societies, I wake up every day thankful that I live in a liberal democracy where the nefarious and intrusive forces of religion have been neutralized. I fear though that a growing dark cloud of totalitarian religious intolerance is descending on our free Western societies. There is perhaps no greater meaning and purpose in life than to combat such retrograde evil.

MATT DILLAHUNTY
SPEAKER / DEBATER / HOST, *THE ATHEIST EXPERIENCE*
AUSTIN, TEXAS

[INTERVIEW] I find joy and meaning all over the place! I don't think there's any externally imposed meaning. I don't even think I would want that. It would be like having someone else pick your major. Don't you want a self-guided life? Isn't there just amazing value in having a self-guided life? And how would you react to someone coming in and saying, "No, this is what you should do with your life!"? I find joy and my life derives meaning from most of the same places anybody else would; religious believers included. I find joy in exploring the world and learning more about where we live. I find joy in interacting with other people; my wife, my family, my friends. I find joy in working with others to make the world a better place.

Life is like its own reward. This idea that some people have that atheists must be nihilists who have no purpose and are all dour all the time, saying, "This life has no meaning and purpose, and why don't we just end it all?" I cannot grasp that. Because it seems just intuitively obvious to me that life is generally preferable to death. That existing is preferable to not existing.

Yes, sometimes there is incredible pain and there may come a time in people's lives where continuing to exist is not preferable to actually ceasing their existence and I'm in favor of people dying with dignity. But while you have life, while you're able to breathe, and eat, and interact, and love, and have sex, and listen to music, and engage in all these wonderful activities, just go for a walk and look around! How could you lack joy and lack meaning or purpose?

Maybe you don't even need to have some grandiose purpose. Maybe your purpose is just, "Hey, let me go explore for a little while and see where I end up tomorrow" That could be purpose enough for most people. What do we do when we're done with the drudgery of the day-to-day work and we take off on vacation? Yes, some people may meticulously plan out their vacations, but a lot of people say, "Let's just go out and take a walk!"

Was that walk wasted? Was the time wasted? Was it joyless? I don't think so.

To me, that's life. It is its own reward.

BETH PRESSWOOD
ARTIST / BIOTECH ASSOCIATE / CO-HOST, *GODLESS BITCHES* PODCAST
AUSTIN, TEXAS

All my life, I was taught that everyone had a "god-shaped hole" in their heart and that no worldly things could ever fill that hole and bring true happiness. Well, I and the other atheists in this book are living proof that no such holes exist. The things we fill our lives with, like love, friendship, and fun are not poor substitutes for god, but are part of the fabric of the true meaning of reality.

My life is a life of love. I have my husband, my kitties, my friends, and my parents. I still love my husband as much as the day I married him. Though there will always be storms in life, I will weather them with him. The love of animals is also a special part of my life. Hana, Dax, Miso, and Bonsai give me affection and comfort on a level that is beyond words and intelligence. My friends give me love too, both the in-person friends and the ones that I've only ever met online. Inventions like Facebook and other parts of the Internet have brought me together with people who share my experiences and values and we have created lasting bonds. I also share love with my parents. Despite our religious differences, my parents still love me and spend time with me. It is bittersweet that I know they have pain because of our differences, but love overcomes our differences.

My life is also a life of fun. The puritanical streak in our society tends to downplay raw pleasure, but fun and pleasure are essential to relieving stress and making our brains work well. One of the things that means the most to me is my crafts. I knit, I bead, and I do resin. Every beautiful thing that comes from my hands is my own creation that I want to share with others, especially by giving handmade gifts to those I love. I would have a hard time listing all the other things I do for fun, but let me say that you haven't lived until you've tubed down a river drinking a margarita in Texas or been to the Smoky Mountains!

Another meaningful, fun, and life-enriching thing I enjoy is Christmas. I mention this because it is extremely important to me and my enthusiasm is a bit rare in the atheist community. I believe that the beautiful evolution of this holiday from pagan origins to Christian ones to a largely secular celebration of love, family, and charity is one that should be celebrated as a triumph. I love the lights, decorations, traditions, making gifts, giving to charity, and the general feeling of connection to others at this time of year.

Left: Beth Presswood and her husband Matt Dillahunty

INDRE VISKONTAS
OPERA SINGER / NEUROSCIENTIST / SCIENCE COMMUNICATOR
SAN FRANCISCO, CALIFORNIA

[INTERVIEW] What gives me joy and what gives my life meaning are two very different categories of things: they are not the same. Joy comes in moments: fleeting, punctate events, ranging from performing with my chamber music ensemble or an opera company, to learning of an accomplishment or winning an audition, to deeply personal moments like the realization that I've fallen in love, or that my brother has a new son. Connecting with other musicians on stage, knowing that the audience will be moved because we are doing something highly creative gives me a lot of joy. But so does finishing a half marathon or reaching some other physical or intellectual goal. It's an addictive feeling, like a high, and my perception of time is warped; things seem to slow down and speed up at the same time. But these moments are fleeting. And as such, I can't rely on them to give my life meaning. Meaning is something that needs to be more pervasive, more constant. It needs to be there even when things aren't going according to plan, when effort seems futile, when life feels unfair, when an innocent is suffering.

Performing, teaching, playing give me joy—it's what I do and what I'm good at—it's important. I don't want to diminish the importance of it, but on the other hand, I also get a lot of joy from my husband throwing me a birthday party or having a great evening with friends at a dinner party or going to a great movie. It's not the same level of joy for sure, but if tomorrow I lost my voice because some accident paralyzes the larynx or I couldn't use my face or hands to express myself, my life would still have meaning.

My life's meaning centers on the relationships with other people in my life. The people whom I love and who love me and who depend on me, or on whom I depend, they are the ones that make life worth living. It's a two-way street. Even if everything else was stripped away, as long as I can connect with the people around me, my life will have meaning.

Ever since I was a kid, I thought I was very lucky: good things just happened to me. I felt fortunate—if there was a raffle, I would buy a ticket. If there was a contest, I would enter. Rationally-speaking, I've certainly lost more contests, grants, raffles, gambles than I have won. But by taking so many chances, I have, indeed, been very lucky. I've won a lot of them and there have been many moments in my life during which I've felt that I was, in some ways, "chosen."

Put those moments together with a desire to create meaning that can pull you through those deeply sad moments, when joy seems like an impossibility, and I can fully understand how a belief in god or other benevolent universal force can be very satisfying. Often in the past, when I was unclear as to which of my, or someone else's, actions caused a happy turn of events in life, it seemed upon reflection that there was a plan in place all along.

And so, when I stopped believing that I was part of some master plan, when I lost my faith, as one might say, I found it very hard at first because all of a sudden, I felt like anytime that I failed or lost or someone died, there was nothing that

I could do to fix it and that it was possible that I had already used up all of my good fortune. Maybe I would never work again—a common fear of freelancers—or maybe everyone I loved would die too soon. When I had faith in a higher power, I chalked it up to the master plan, believing that it would eventually turn out for the best. That's a hard thing to let go of.

But now I feel empowered by the knowledge that there is no plan, and it's up to me and it's up to those around me to do the things that we want to do and make the plans that we need to accomplish our goals. All of a sudden, I feel like wow, the world really is my oyster. I can choose any path that I want. It isn't pre-determined, and I have to be more careful about the choices that I make because they will affect the choices I will have in the future. That's a lot of pressure. But, I used to stumble through life feeling like everything will work out just because, and now I'm much more intellectual about the choices I make, knowing that the consequences and future opportunities are up to me. Living in San Francisco helps a lot: support for California dreams is strong here, and the creative community is vast and closely-knit at the same time. There seems to be an unending supply of opportunities. And quality is rewarded with a captive audience.

That's what brings us together and gives our lives more than just moments of joy: it gives us meaning.

JAMES CROFT

DOCTORAL CANDIDATE,
HARVARD GRADUATE SCHOOL OF EDUCATION
CAMBRIDGE, MASSACHUSETTS

[INTERVIEW] Robert Ingersoll, "The Great Agnostic"—a Humanist orator after whom I model my activism—once said, "The glory of science is, that it is freeing the soul, breaking the mental manacles, getting the brain out of bondage, giving courage to thought, filling the world with mercy, justice, and joy."

For ten years I battled to free my soul, struggling to free my brain from self-imposed bondage. Finally, on Friday, March 19th, 2010, I broke the mental manacles I had shackled myself with, and exploded out of the closet. In the oldest gay bar in the country—Café Lafitte in Exile, New Orleans—I finally accepted who I am.

The sense of joy, power, and fulfillment I felt at that moment, and for months afterward, is difficult to describe. My heart was aflame, my veins running with liquid gold, and the world was fizzing with new possibilities. I felt strong, in control of myself, more capable than I had felt before: my work as an activist and public speaker really took off only after I had found the courage of thought that comes with self-acceptance. And I was *happy*. I was joyful every day, for months! I skipped through life as if on clouds.

I draw two lessons from my coming out struggle, and from the decade of my life I spent preoccupied with it. First, I recognize that life is precious, and short, and that in this one life we have, we must strive to squeeze the most out of every single moment ("comer el mundo"). There is no time to waste trying to be someone we are not. Second, I realize that my life feels most joyful and meaningful when I am working to unlock the power inside others, freeing them from cages of the mind. The strength I found within myself when I finally accepted my sexuality is strength we all can have, and I have dedicated my life to helping other people find that power.

This is the thread that connects all aspects of my life: I make meaning in my life by helping people fulfill their full potential. When I feel like I've been useful to someone, when I've unlocked in them the belief that they can achieve something they didn't think they could achieve before, or have expanded their horizons to encompass some new idea—that's when I feel most joyful.

I find my life's purpose in freeing the soul—just like Robert Ingersoll.

Photo: Croft with Robert Ingersoll

RUTHLIN ZEPHYR
BIOLOGY STUDENT, STONY BROOK UNIVERSITY
LONG ISLAND, NEW YORK

When I was a kid growing up in Haiti, I imagined the world as a well-structured place where the grown-ups understood everything and were wisely guided in their endeavors. At least, that's the impression I got, since the adults had apparent answers for all the questions that I had as child.

As I grew older, I started to become more and more disillusioned with the world as I increasingly began to see through my assumptions and through the pretenses of the world. I started seeing the world as a place filled with uncertain people swimming in confusion, misunderstandings, and false beliefs—many of which, contribute to the suffering of the world. Witnessing this problem urged me to dedicate myself to learning as much as I could about the world and about myself, so that I could become a helping hand in reducing the misery in the world.

As I mature, I intend to get a better grasp of human psychology in order to help people rid themselves of unnecessary stress and hardship. I also desire to become more knowledgeable on matters that have to do with technology and engineering. I long to contribute to the growing scientific body of knowledge, and also to work with new technology that can help people to lead better, healthier, and more enriched lives.

To me, life doesn't need to have some grand intrinsic meaning. Well, I don't think it does. Living is, in many ways, like a party which is enjoyable in itself, without the need of some majestic purpose. I get plenty of joy in daily pleasures, like listening to music or eating a delicious meal. However, even greater satisfaction is to be had in pursuing goals aimed at making life better for everyone. That is my persistent motivation. It gives my life a firm sense of purpose and definite direction to aspire to be a contributor to the betterment of the lives of those living now and those who have yet to come into existence. I am therefore very excited to be a voice in helping to raise the awareness of our society and also in helping to forge a more refined attitude towards atheists as we move forward.

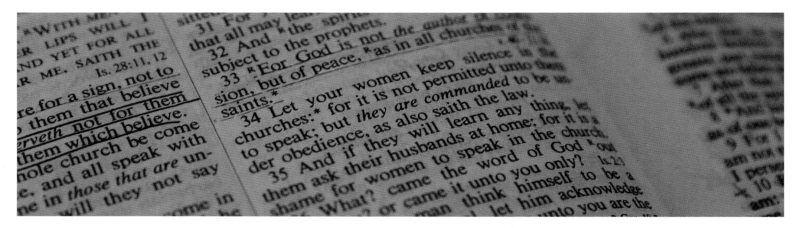

TERESA MACBAIN
FORMER METHODIST MINISTER
TALLAHASSEE, FLORIDA

[INTERVIEW] I was raised as a Baptist preacher's daughter; I was very much in love with God and church. I studied the Bible and did everything I could to further myself along toward learning more about God. I felt like I was called by God to be a minister when I was six years old, but being a girl pretty much closed the door on me being any type of minister besides teaching children or women's ministry. The only option I had as a woman was the foreign ministry field. I could teach—this is what I was taught—natives in Africa, New Zealand, or maybe Aborigines in Australia. That was the lifestyle I was raised in. It was very conservative and I continued in that vein for many, many years. I eventually worked through the theology issues regarding women, and came to believe that the Bible did allow women to be pastors. So I became a Methodist pastor and served in that capacity for many years.

About three to five years ago, I began questioning. I was trying to find answers. I wanted to resolve some of these questions so that I'd be a better pastor and a better Christian. As I worked through the Bible, over many years, I began to realize that I didn't believe any of it any longer. I left the ministry and came out on March 26, 2012 at the American Atheists National Convention.

I had lived in a particular world, surrounded by church people, and spoke a different language. In the church, we had our own style of music, our own style of communication, thought patterns, everything. My husband was in the military, and when we would move, the very first thing that we did was to look for a church. We then searched for a home near the church. The church was the center of everything. Our family instantly connected to the church community. Immediately we were welcomed. It wasn't just a church to me...it was my home. So when I came out as an atheist, it felt like I stepped off of a cliff. Without the religious life that filled every corner of my world, I didn't know who I was. Maybe that's not a good way to say it, but I definitely didn't know

how to live apart from it. I didn't know where to go to make friends. I didn't know how to find relationships because all of a sudden, after I came out, all of my relationships were gone, with the exception of my husband and my kids. Some family members came around after that, but in that moment and in the first few months, there was nothing. It was just me. I was just out there by myself, and for somebody who's really social, that's hard to take.

When you're in a religious community, especially for me anyway, everything revolves around God. Your joy is found in the Lord. Your meaning is found in serving God. This was the meaning of life to me. So when you walk away from that, you really have to discover what is truth, what is reality. I told myself, "There has to be something more than just serving God or loving God." So for me the meaning of life, or the meaning in life, is helping people and loving people, being in community with others, reaching out to my fellow humans in their time of need, helping them to grow and develop, to be strong, and "be all that they can be," as the Army would say.

That has been my true meaning of life, for all these years. That's who I am. A person who loves others, who gives themselves in helping and nurturing people, and that brings me joy. When I can go and speak at a conference, great! Wonderful! I love to speak in front of people. But the real joy for me is when someone comes up to me and they want to just sit down and share their struggle with me. Maybe they ask me for advice or maybe they don't, but just knowing that they have a safe place and can talk to someone who has been there, that gives me great joy. I know that my life has meaning because I'm helping someone. Helping them to walk down this very, very difficult path.

When I came out as an atheist, the loss of the community and the way of living that I had known all my life was like losing everything all at once.

The thing that surprised me however, was the way that the secular community rallied around me. People that I didn't know were friending me on Facebook, they're sending me messages, constantly asking how I'm doing, and having conversations with me. It wasn't out of any kind of sense of, "let's feel her out and make sure she's serious about this" or "let's make sure she's not a plant, an enemy agent, or covert operative." It was all very genuine, very heartfelt. "I know what you're going through, I've been there." "I remember when I first came out. Here are some things that worked for me." It was community; real community.

Community exists, and by our own nature, we want it, and I experienced it. Everything I've been through over the last 11 months has been about a network of freethinkers rallying around me, supporting my family and me. I remember in Tallahassee, after I came back, the Tallahassee atheists had a meet-up. They invited me to attend, so I went. It was fun, I enjoyed it, and I felt—even though I didn't know the people very well—like I was one of them. They encouraged me to bring my husband, even though he's still a Christian. They didn't care what he believed. It was an understanding of, "yeah, we think differently on that one topic, but we're still humans, and we can still care for one another." Off we went, every week, to drink coffee, talk about science fiction books or fantasy novels, or whatever. He'd always find a group that he'd talk with, and I would be my normal socialite self and buzz around talking to everyone. Even after I moved to New Jersey and he stayed in Florida, he went to the atheist meet-ups on Sunday morning, instead of going to church. They represent the kind of supportive, caring people who came surprisingly to our family. I never knew and never really dreamed that "evil atheists" could do those sorts of things. It was very shocking, and very surprising...a nice surprise.

BRIAN DUNNING

SCIENCE WRITER / HOST AND PRODUCER OF THE *SKEPTOID* PODCAST
LAGUNA NIGUEL, CALIFORNIA

Although I certainly make no secret of the fact that I am without religious convictions of any kind, I avoid the word *atheist* like the plague. It means too many things to too many different people, most of them negative, and I've always hoped to have as little negativity as possible in the work that I do.

When most people look at religion, they see a comforting belief in which they have faith, often including hope for an afterlife. I respect that they feel that way and I'm glad they have what they get from it. But when I look at religion for myself, I see a childishly absurd magical sky wizard, a lot of provably untrue world history, and a book that has to be interpreted with deliberate cherry-picking to be seen as a positive guide for anything. I have no use for those things, but that's my business. It's irrelevant to the things I choose to share.

I prefer to communicate the excitement of discovery and learning, whatever the subject matter: history, urban legends, popular mysteries, ghost stories. There is so much to learn in these subject areas, all of it marvelous. One of the challenges I face is that it's hard to get someone to consider a neat optical effect (for example) if they're unwilling to look beyond their insistence that what they're seeing is a literal ghost or spirit.

Helping someone strip away a set of beliefs that wrongly characterizes their own world can be a good thing, as long as you follow it up with the wonder of what's really going on. Don't just pull

the curtain aside unless you're also going to show them what's behind it. I find it useless to simply say, "Your cherished belief is wrong." That, in a nutshell, is why I loathe the term *atheist*: too many people see it merely as a negative, thuggish belief system.

I'm always pleased that I so frequently receive e-mails from Christians, Jews, Muslims, and others who tell me how much they enjoy my show, and how much they appreciate that I don't make fun of them or insult them the way some other science and skeptical resources tend to. To me, that's a sign that I'm doing something right. And I don't for a second consider myself to be tolerating a lack of skepticism, and shaping my message to conform to others' beliefs. Not at all. With every project I produce, I try to nudge everyone in the right direction, toward an appreciation of how awesome it is to learn what's really happening. I'm trying to nudge them with honey, not with a stick. If their experience is good, they may just come back for more; and hopefully they exercise their fundamental right to choose to apply scientific skepticism to other aspects of their lives, as they see fit to do so. I know that the real world can provide all the wonder and opportunities for self-improvement anyone could ever want.

VALERIE TARICO
PSYCHOLOGIST / WRITER
SEATTLE, WASHINGTON

Some years ago I chanced on a question posed by poet Mary Oliver: "Tell me, what is it you want to do with your one wild and precious life?" Her words startled and delighted me. *One wild and precious life.* During my years as a born-again Christian, life was simply a prelude to an Iron Age eternity of either singing God's praises or suffering damnation and torture. Now having emerged from the walled fortress of Bible belief, I was faced with a wonder, a universe minutely and ever so briefly conscious in me, filled with curiosities and beauties and loves made all the more poignant by their transience.

For me no art in the world is more beautiful than a blade of grass. Picture this: You are lying face down on a damp lawn, summer sun soaking through the back of your t-shirt, smells of your own salty arms and the steamy garden on any breath of air that tickles your face. Birdsong flits in and out of your awareness. You lift your head and look at the grass in front of you, just inches away. You focus in on one blade, following its lines up to the tip or down to where it disappears into the tangle. The greens are translucent and opaque, almost chartreuse then almost black. And you know that no matter how close or far you look, each ordinary elegant blade will be perfectly intricate, and that beneath the spider web of matter lies an echo of the vast emptiness of the universe itself.

To quote the words of Tim Minchin: "Isn't this enough? Just this world? Just this beautiful, complex, wonderfully unfathomable, *natural* world? How does it so fail to hold our attention

that we have to diminish it with the invention of cheap, man-made Myths and Monsters?"

This beautiful, complex world gives me both joy and purpose. The joys are large and small: Two kind, curious daughters and a husband who has been my best friend for over 20 years. Three ridiculous chickens that watch through the window while I write. A tradition of spending August unplugged at a cabin in the San Juan Islands where life takes on an ancestral rhythm of planting, mowing, pitting myself against the waves in a small rowboat, and lingering with friends and songs into the night.

But life's joy is counterbalanced by the world's need, and sometimes my home and community feel like Rivendell in a world under siege. When forced once to summarize my life purpose in a single sentence, I wrote this: My mission is to tend the well-being of the intricate web of creation that gave me birth and the well-being of my fellow humans within that web. My various projects ranging from the Wisdom Commons, *Trusting Doubt*, and AwayPoint, to my fierce advocacy for reproductive rights and technologies, all seek to serve this mission. I love knowing that I am a part of a vast, largely invisible network of people working toward the same end. A minister once asked me about my spiritual community, and I floundered for words, because for me, spiritual community is this: people, whether or not I shall ever meet them, who give themselves to the challenge of healing and protecting our unfathomably wonderful world.

Following page: Tarico (center) with her daughters Marley (right) and Brynn (left) holding Tegan the chicken

DANIEL DENNETT
PHILOSOPHER AND COGNITIVE SCIENTIST, TUFTS UNIVERSITY
MEDFORD, MASSACHUSETTS

[INTERVIEW] There are two ways of looking at the source of meaning. There's the old-fashioned way, which is the trickle-down theory of meaning. Our lives can't have meaning unless we're the lesser products of something even more meaningful than we are: God. We're God's creations, God's army, God's tools, his toys, his playthings. That's what gives us meaning. We inherit from the Big Meaner.

The other way of looking at it is the bubble-up theory of meaning, which is that the universe starts off without any meaning and there really is no point to it, but it's possible for life to evolve, and it does. We eventually show up—and we are meaning-makers, and we care. Initially we just care because that comes along with our instincts as part of our biology. But as we think and reflect and care, we begin to move away from our biological roots and things begin to matter more to us. And what could have more meaning than the things that matter the most to us? That's who we are.

We can meet in rational exploration and mutual persuasion and decide which things are really important. Do we all agree? Now maybe there's always going to be a few outliers, people that just don't get the point of it or go their own way. Okay, as long as they don't hurt us. But pretty much there's agreement about what ought to be done, what a good life is, what a good life for others is. There's always room for improvement, but once you've got that basic agreement—and that's homegrown ethics, not an edict from on high—you don't have to be told by an eternal being what's right and wrong. You figure out what right and wrong is.

Then you're motivated to act on this. I look around the world and see so many wonderful things that I love and enjoy and benefit from, whether it's art or music or clothing or food and all the rest. And I'd like to add a little to that goodness. Rather than thanking God, this nonexistent benefactor,

the way to thank the human beings who created all this is to create a little bit more goodness if I can, and add to the goodness in the world.

In 2006, I had an aortic dissection, which is usually fatal, and fatal within minutes or hours. I was extremely lucky that some scar tissue left over from my previous heart operation wrapped itself around my aorta like duct tape and kept it together long enough to get me into the hospital and into surgery. (So today I have a Dacron aorta and a carbon fiber aortic valve, which makes me a little bit bionic.)

Now, heart operations where they use the heart and lung machine are notoriously likely to cause lots of little mini-strokes in your brain because they kick up a lot of debris, which clogs up the capillaries. So I went into that operation worried that I might come out, as one says, a "pump head." I did not want to be a "pump head."

And so the surgeons—I'm very grateful for this—knowing my particular concern about this, brainwashed me literally. After the operation they reversed the flow of blood through my brain, switched the hoses so they pumped it in the veins and out the arteries to flush out any little junk that was sticking in the capillaries. I was very relieved to learn of this when I awoke from surgery, but I wanted to see, as soon as possible, if I was now a "pump head." So with my trusty laptop right there in the hospital I started writing the piece, *Thank Goodness*, mainly to see if I still had my marbles. That was my main goal and I was very grateful to discover I could still think and write.

I was also amused by the fact that some of my close friends actually had said to me, with a little bit of a blush, that they'd been praying for me. And I decided I had to have some fun with this. So I didn't actually say to them what I had the urge to say: "thanks, but did you also sacrifice a goat?" I didn't say that. It would have been too

rude. But I could talk about it later. I appreciated the fact they cared enough, they thought enough and it was important to them. But I really wanted to tell them to think about what they had said. You know that I know that intercessory prayer doesn't work. In fact there's good scientific evidence that it doesn't work. So if you actually take this seriously, you're doing something that is sort of an affront to science and everything I stand for. I appreciate your temptation to do it and I honor that, but if you actually want to help, there are better things you can do. You can plant a tree. You can send money to Oxfam. There are lots and lots and lots of things you can do. I'd rather have you do that then think that time and energy spent praying for me is actually helping. It just isn't and I wanted to make that very clear.

I also wanted to write about the people in the hospital around me that struck me as just wonderful. I may have been somewhat under the influence of sedatives or something but I was impressed with their conscientiousness and their teamwork, the care they took, not just to do their own job but also to check on each other and to help each other. I thought: wouldn't it be nice if academia worked that way, which it pretty much doesn't.

And I also thought: when people give thanks to God for surviving, why don't they thank the ones who are really responsible? The people around them and their predecessors who put some goodness into the world that now is actually helping them. For instance, Allan Cormack, my late colleague at Tufts, proud winner of the Nobel Prize for the CAT scan. I know he can't hear me because he's not in heaven because there is no such place. But his CAT scan saved my life. So thank you, Allan.

JEN PEEPLES
AEROSPACE ENGINEER / CO-HOST, *THE ATHEIST EXPERIENCE, GODLESS BITCHES* PODCAST
AUSTIN, TEXAS

[INTERVIEW] There are many things out there that give my life meaning and purpose. I have a job where I investigate and have the satisfaction of solving some truly difficult problems. One of the things that gets me up in the morning is the fact that I don't know everything. I will never know everything. There's so much more out there than I can ever get my hands around.

And it's all just waiting for me to explore. It's like, "What do I want to explore today?" And if I were still religious, going by what my family members who are still religious tell me, I would believe that it's all laid out for me already. Everything is already decided. And to me, that would feel like just going through the motions. What are you doing here on the planet if it's all decided? Why are you here?

For me, there's this whole world of possibility out there. I think about some of the things I've experienced in my life. For example, when I was in Germany we'd be flying on an instrument flight plan, and we would pop up above the cloud deck. You can see the clouds a thousand feet below you. We used to request a lower altitude so that we could just get our helicopter skids in the clouds, so you're flying along just on top of the clouds. It's almost like flying on a cloud itself.

Watch the sunrise doing that!

HEMANT MEHTA
HIGH SCHOOL MATH TEACHER / BLOGGER AT *THE FRIENDLY ATHEIST*
NAPERVILLE, ILLINOIS

I began to lose my faith in God around the same time my family got Internet access. It's weird to say this now, but those events weren't related. Even though the Internet didn't cause my atheism, it was the place where I went to learn more about what atheism entailed. At the time, there weren't blogs or easy-to-read books about the subject. There were just a handful of websites whose owners discussed why believing in God made no sense. Those websites looked hideous, like the rantings of crazy people. But I still read them, partly because my options were so limited. The more I did that, the more I realized they were on to something. That meant that either I was also crazy, or we were all right.

I was a high school freshman when all of this happened. I didn't have any close friends who were nonreligious, I didn't know that it was possible to start an atheist group at my school, and I didn't have any outlets where I could talk about my newfound beliefs—at least none I knew about. That may be why I'm so passionate about talking and writing about atheism today, and why I want to make sure young atheists, especially, have the resources they need to explore their religious faith (or lack thereof). I know how much it would have meant to me to have that kind of information at my fingertips after I gave up my religion, and I want to make sure students today

don't have to go through that same drought. I can't take credit for all of this, but over the past ten years we've seen the number of campus atheist groups go from the low double digits to the mid-triple digits. And we haven't seen any big signs of that growth slowing down.

In a way—and I realize how old I sound when I say this—I'm jealous of what teenagers have nowadays: Online communities to discuss their atheism (and, if they want, rant about religion). Resources to create their own atheist groups and network with others around the country. Access to books that both educate them about atheism-related issues and inspire them to take action against religious privilege. A seemingly endless number of blogs written by atheists talking about current events from a non-theistic perspective.

More than anything, they have the knowledge that they are not alone. There are atheists everywhere, in their communities and perhaps even in their schools. The past decade has seen atheism become mainstream, popular, and more accessible. The next decade needs to see that growth harnessed into political and social power so that being an atheist and promoting reason and critical thinking isn't seen as a liability, but a virtue. I have hope that today's young atheists will turn that fantasy into a reality.

MICHAEL NUGENT
WRITER / CHAIRPERSON, ATHEIST IRELAND
DUBLIN, IRELAND

[INTERVIEW] We get joy and meaning from absorption in activities that we enjoy doing, that we do just for the sake of doing. We also get joy and meaning from our personal relationships, like my relationships with my family, particularly my relationship with my late wife Anne, who I loved dearly. We spent loads of time together not just as a couple; we also shared the same interests politically and in an activist sense. And there is also a general sense of meaning that each individual gives to themselves. For my wife and me, it was campaigning for a more tolerant, compassionate, empathetic, secular Ireland, campaigning both against the problems caused by the Catholic Church and the problems caused by IRA and loyalist terrorism. Ireland had religion and nationalism and terrorism entangled together for so long that it was a terrible mess. Thankfully, a lot of that is now closer to being part of Ireland's past than it was 20 or 30 years ago, so that's a good thing.

While Anne was dying, we did a range of different things. Because she was on chemotherapy, we couldn't do things that lasted a long time, as she would have to be back every so often for chemotherapy. We went on a lot of short trips abroad, like we'd go on weekends abroad to Paris or Scandinavia or England. We went to visit a lot of friends that we hadn't seen in a while. We also just did fairly mundane things: on the days that Anne was very weak because of the chemotherapy, we would just sit at home and watch box sets of DVDs of television programs that we had liked over the years, or our favorite movies. And those times, although very mundane, were very meaningful to the extent that in retrospect, the time that I miss Anne most now is when I'm watching television because I'm reliving those times that we were just sitting there watching those box sets of DVDs.

My cat Boris is the king of not only the six cats in this house but also of the area. I think he gets fed at 90% of the houses on the road. He occasionally gets himself lost by being too friendly and wandering a little bit off and losing his sense of direction. One of the times he got lost, I met a guy living in an old folks home nearby and he was helping me look for Boris. We were chatting away, and ironically enough—given that Anne and I spent a lot of our life campaigning against the IRA—I eventually realized that this guy was a former senior IRA man. And he told me he was going to make it his mission to find Boris. And he rang us up a week later, saying that he had found Boris. I went down to his flat and, sure enough, it was Boris. I asked "where was he?" and he said one of the other guys in the complex had taken him in, "but I persuaded him to give him back."

I'm a vegetarian and an animal lover, and I believe that all species on the planet are equally as valuable as human beings. I think that every day we can do something that brings our knowledge and our ethics a little bit further. Every generation, we find out more and more and more about the universe, how it operates naturally. We discover how parochial the religious stories about humans being in charge of everything are. In our tiny part of the known universe of a hundred billion galaxies, each of which has a hundred billion stars like our sun, the idea that all of it exists for the benefit of humans on planet Earth is just absurd in the extreme. So we just do our little bit on our little planet to try and make things a bit better every day. And although what I do on any given day is insignificant in the overall scheme of things, the cumulative impact of everybody doing that on an ongoing basis is what gradually increases the quality of life from generation to generation, for future generations.

REBECCA NEWBERGER GOLDSTEIN
PHILOSOPHER / NOVELIST
BOSTON & TRURO, MASSACHUSETTS

Photo: Rebecca Newberger Goldstein and Steven Pinker at their home on Cape Cod

[INTERVIEW] I have a kind of adulation of genius of every sort. I love the feeling of being overwhelmed by what the human mind can produce. Whenever I read a remarkable poem, or I listen to a piece of remarkable music, or I understand a piece of remarkable mathematics, and I know that this came from people—with all of their pettiness and smallness and yet they were able to achieve the remarkable—I'm inspired by that. The sense of being overwhelmed by what individual minds can produce in whatever field, is to me magnificent. Humankind is always offering evidence that it's better than it is and also worse than it is. Both offer chilling experiences, awesome in their own ways, awesomely terrible and awesomely inspiring.

Some religious people can't understand how someone can be moral without a God. It is a huge question for a lot of people who can't conceptualize what could possibly ground morality, make the difference between a right and wrong action, without a transcendent source. Morality is mysterious to us because it seems not to describe just what is the case, but what ought to be the case. David Hume said very famously that you can't derive an "ought" from an "is." Now what we observe, and what science tells us, are facts about what is the case. So how do we

derive from these facts any truths about about what ought to be the case? It seems mysterious, trans-empirical. Its mysteriousness seems to require a mysterious, trans-empirical source, namely God.

And yet another problem, on top of this first mystery: Even if there are these objective facts about how you ought to behave, why would anybody obey these "ought"s if there's not the Great Enforcer imposing cosmic repercussions? Won't you do whatever you can get away with? Isn't that the reasonable thing to do, never mind that there are these objective "ought"s? These are all questions that moral philosophers have been contemplating and making progress with ever since there's been moral philosophy, ever since Plato and Aristotle. When we read the bible, we interpret it as, "Oh it can't really mean this! We don't really want to stone an adulterer. We don't really think it's okay that you can get slaves as long as they're from foreign countries." So we're re-interpreting with the backing of millennia of moral reasoning which have slowly worked to change our moral sensibilities. It's been torturously slow progress. Why did it take us so long to realize that every human has the right to a life of dignity and self-fulfillment? But yet, slow as it has been, progress has been made. So even among religious people, they're not getting

morality from the good book. They're reading the good book in the light of accumulated moral reasoning that has reshaped what seems intuitive and obvious. They're reinterpreting the good book so that it doesn't clash with hard-won "intuitions" that those who wrote the good book lacked.

Some religious people also feel that you miss a kind of transcendence, a getting out of yourself, in a life without God. I think it's very natural to put the experiences we have of transcendence, an almost ecstatic experience that one can have, into religious language. That language comes very naturally to us. It's already there, ready to be utilized to express these anomalous experiences that lift us out of the here and now. I'm quite prone to this kind of experience. But there's nothing exclusively religious about it. It has something to do with all the processes that make us able to think objectively and get outside of ourselves. It's taking those processes to their logical extreme. Math can do it to us, music can do it to us, starry nights can do it to us. These are secular ways of achieving transcendence, of feeling lifted into a grand perspective. It's a sense of being awed by existence that almost obliterates the self. Religious people think of it as an essentially religious experience but it's not. It's an essentially human experience.

STEVEN PINKER
COGNITIVE SCIENTIST
BOSTON & TRURO, MASSACHUSETTS

[INTERVIEW] Without a God or afterlife, there is more of an impetus to cherish the people you love while they are here, to realize that they aren't going to be here forever, and not to squander opportunities to enjoy them and let them enjoy you. Also, as terrifying, inconceivable, unacceptable and horrific as death is—we're grownups. I don't want someone to treat me like a child and pretend that it's not the case, as when we tell them "The goldfish that's floating in the bowl is actually up in heaven with the other goldfish." You grow out of that, and as horrible as death is, it's better knowing it exists than pretending that it doesn't, at least over the long term. Every day, to be sure, we pretend that death doesn't exist as we live our lives. But we also, at crucial moments, remind ourselves that "life is short," and think about what that cliché impels us to do. It impels us to bury the hatchet in a pointless dispute, to see an aging relative that you might put off indefinitely, to extend a gesture of affection to a loved one. If you're not going to be around forever, then you treat every moment with the specialness it deserves.

I know that many people also think that if there isn't some divine plan you're carrying out, it means you're condemned to a life of selfish hedonism, that there's no reason to do anything that doesn't give you pleasure or serve your own interests. This is also a failure to think things through. As soon as you're engaged with other people (as all of us except Robinson Crusoe are) you've got to live your life in a way that takes into account the interests of others, if for no other reason than you want other people to take your interests into account. But also, as you start to use your own mind, you start to realize that there are things that are bigger than you. They're not divine, but they will certainly outlive you: the truths of science and mathematics, the existence of the world, your children, the consequences of your actions. Even if you aren't around to see those things for yourself, they make a difference in your life as you plan it and live it. As an analogy, when you practice a sports move like a tennis serve or golf swing, you worry about the follow-through, about how the swing continues after it's met the ball. It's not that the follow-through can actually affect the way the ball travels—the future can't affect the past—but as you plan the entire swing knowing there's a follow-through, and anticipating it, it changes the way you execute the action. And likewise, knowing there is a world that will outlive you, there are people whose well-being depends on how you live your life, affects the way you live your life, whether or not you directly experience those effects. You want to be the kind of person who has the larger view, who takes other people's interests into account, who's dedicated to principles that you can justify, like justice, knowledge, truth, beauty and morality. And you live your life differently knowing those principles exist.

There are a lot of ideas that are difficult for a human mind to grasp. They pertain to something that extends beyond our own everyday experience, the infinite, the origin of time, the nature of conscious awareness. Where does space end? Where does time begin? And you're apt to project that onto religious narratives. But you can easily subtract the part about a conscious being in the sky, and still retain an appreciation of issues that are bigger than any of us. It's true that the language of religion often comes naturally to us when we're in that mode. That's why physicists talk about the God Particle, the mind of God, how would God see the situation—even though by doing that of course the physicists are very clear they're not actually referring to God.

I'm inspired by the quest to understand the world, in particular human beings: what makes us tick. It's a pursuit that is endlessly fascinating, bigger than anything that I myself could hope to achieve. It's an honor and inspiration to be part of a community that's trying to do that, to answer questions like how does the mind work? Where does language come from? What makes a system intelligent? What makes us cooperate? What makes us compete? Where does love come from? Why do we have a sense of beauty? It's an endless set of questions about human nature that will go on long after me, but which I feel privileged to be a part of while I'm alive.

WILLIAM DAVID MYERS
HISTORIAN / WRITER
NEW YORK, NEW YORK

[INTERVIEW] Being alive was not a decision. It was simply a lucky happenstance that I had no control over. Even my parents had relatively little control over it, aside from the lucky act of creation itself. So the fact that I am alive is not meaningful in any cosmic sense, but it is something that I experience and enjoy every day—that I look forward to every day.

Meaning is a difficult term to use because I think the universe is pointless in any ultimate way, and yet for the short time that we're here, we invest it with significance for our own lives. We give fulfillment and satisfaction to one another and ourselves. This is partly because it's pleasurable just to be and to experience others, and partly because biologically our nature is to interact and to move forward—biologically, we are social creatures, and that is the context of our sense of what is significant.

Focusing on this world—concentrating on the beauties and joys of this world, of the life that I have—brings me more sense of beauty and more meaning and more completeness than seeing the world as somehow reflecting the will of or contingent on the whims of some deity, someone beyond us. At least this is true for me.

I don't put off friendships with the idea that there will be something more in the future. I don't put off what I think is beautiful in this world as a down payment on something better in another world. I don't feel like I'm doing layaway with my eternity here. I really do believe that I want, in this life, to experience it as much as possible, to have as much meaning as I can make of it, as much beauty as it can provide. That makes a big difference to me and how I deal with the world.

It makes a difference in friendship. I know at this point in my life I'm very conscious if I'm with friends, say, in New York, in Munich, or walking with students or deeply religious people on the Camino de Santiago. To spend an evening with friends, the night spread out before us, and to enjoy, intensely, all of the things that human interchange can bring is, to me, really quite meaningful and I don't think of it in reference to something else.

I like the idea that this is a moment that will be gone in an instant and won't come again. Yet the moment is full and doesn't need anything else. It's not more complete because there's a God involved, or not involved. It's not more sufficient because this will be a memory I will have long after my death when I'm gazing down from eternity. It is simply *now*, and I think *that* for me, is enough. And, at the end of the day, should God appear, well, I will be pleasantly surprised. But I will also have a lot of questions.

JAMES WATSON
MOLECULAR BIOLOGIST
CO-DISCOVERER OF THE STRUCTURE OF DNA
NOBEL PRIZE FOR PHYSIOLOGY OR MEDICINE, 1962
COLD SPRING HARBOR, NEW YORK

By early adolescence, both Francis Crick
and I had stopped going to our respective
Congregational and Catholic churches. Accepting
the dictates of a Christian God who spoke to us
though the Bible or Catechism was not in our
natures. Neither of us saw reason to believe
in the existence of a superior being who, after
creating the universe, filled it with human beings
destined to best move through their lives accepting
his existence. Even before we first met in 1951,
neither Francis or I saw reason to believe that
creation or continued existence of life demanded
more than the harmonious working together of
the already existing basic laws of physics and
chemistry.

MICHAEL SHERMER

FOUNDER AND PUBLISHER OF *SKEPTIC* MAGAZINE
LOS ANGELES, CALIFORNIA

[INTERVIEW] What gives my life joy and meaning? Family, my daughter, my sweetheart, my friends, productive work, and just engaging the world in a proactive, energetic, exciting way. To me, that's it. Every day. Play hard, work hard, and love hard. I just have good meaningful relationships with friends and family, and I do productive things and have fun. That's enough, I think. It's plenty. I don't see why people seem to think they need more. They all say it, and I'm not sure if they really believe it or really even thought much about it. They say it because they heard other people say it, I think.

Visits to observatories resonate deeply with me. They are kind of the cathedrals of our time. Chartres Cathedral, Notre Dame, St. Paul's Cathedral... they are magnificent structures, but right up here, just above my house there is Mt. Wilson Observatory where Hubble discovered the expanding universe. It's right there, above Los Angeles, right near where I live. It's incredible to think of how important this scientific cathedral is to our understanding of the world. You can hike right up to it, and stand inside that huge dome and see the big 100-inch telescope. It's just awe inspiring. It's better than art and architecture and statues and cathedrals, not only because it's all that wrapped up into one package, but because it has the virtue of actually finding something out that's true, something that exists outside of our imagination. Our cathedrals and our art—this is all human imagination, which is fantastic, but science does one better. It does all of that and it goes and searches for something that's actually out there, and separate from our brain.

I was once a believer. I was an evangelical Christian for about seven years. I became a Christian in high school. I accepted Jesus as my savior. John 3:16—"For God so loved the world, he gave his only begotten son." Et cetera. But in my case it was not the influence of my parents, it was my peer group who were really into that stuff. It was the 1970s and I just sort of followed along, then I got into it, and really took it seriously. I read the Bible carefully and took courses in the Old Testament and the New Testament and the life of Christ and the writings of C.S. Lewis. I went to Pepperdine University to major in theology, but I switched to psychology because I figured someday I'd have to get a job. I wanted to be a college professor, and to do you have to have a PhD and to get a doctorate in theology, you have to master Hebrew, Greek, Aramaic and Latin and I could barely get through Spanish. I figured I better do something I can actually master. So I switched to experimental psychology, where I

learned the scientific method. Carefully controlled experiments and the whole principle of having evidence for your claims really contradicted a lot of the ways I saw theologians and philosophers think. I resonated more with the scientific way of thinking and eventually abandoned my beliefs.

When you're in the Christian bubble, surrounded by fellow Christians, everything makes perfect sense and it's all internally coherent and logical and everything happens for a reason. But when you're not in the bubble, which I wasn't when I went to graduate school—nobody was religious, or maybe they were, I don't know, it didn't make any difference, it didn't come up—I realized that when I didn't believe anymore, it didn't really matter. No one really cared, other than my siblings and parents, who were a bit relieved that I quit witnessing to them for Jesus. I wasn't married. I didn't belong to a big church community that I'd be ousted from. I wouldn't lose any friends really, so it was easy for me to quit believing. I can see why it's harder for other people in different stages of their lives, though, especially where they come from these small towns. I live in Los Angeles where we're surrounded by atheists and agnostics and freethinkers and Deepak Chopra fans and gays and lesbians and blacks and Mexicans—we just have all forms of diversity of people and beliefs here, so it doesn't matter and nobody really cares what you believe. I'm more sympathetic of course to people that do not live in big liberal cities like L.A. So when we get letters from people saying, "Oh man I've read your magazine and your books, and you have no idea, it's like everybody in this town goes to church, every one of them— everybody I work with, my whole family believes— I'm alone." It's like, wow, it's a different world that we inhabit in academia or in big cities.

Don't put off for later what you could do now. I've violated that too much, you know, in terms of relationships or sports, more academic research I should've started earlier, should've done things earlier. It just seems like when you're 18 you have infinite time, and before you know it, you're in your 50s and you're like, "Holy moly, I better get cracking here." Not that I'm not an unproductive person, but I can say definitely that I should've been a little more foresightful, but that's the point. When you're 18, you're not. That's why you're 18.

The bottom line for me is to live life to the fullest in the here-and-now instead of a hoped-for hereafter, and make every day count in some meaningful way and do something—no matter how small it is— to make the world a better place.

MIRANDA TRADEWELL
MEDICAL WRITER
TORONTO, ONTARIO, CANADA

At one point I was a firm believer in God—a born-again Christian, even. College, friends, and a strong education in science stripped me of that over several years. Freeing myself from the burden of dogmatic beliefs was incredible; I no longer had to reconcile or justify my belief system with the rest of the world. I was free to learn, to observe, and to try and see the world and the universe as they really are. After my undergrad and a bit of travelling, I started my PhD. I have always loved to learn and to read, and they actually paid me to do these things, although it was also a lot of work.

My desire to help people through research led me to study the causes of ALS (Amyotrophic Lateral Sclerosis; aka Lou Gehrig's Disease). I spent nine years researching this disease, earning my PhD, getting married, then starting a postdoctoral fellowship and having our two children.

My family gives me my purpose in life; together they have made me a better, stronger, and hopefully kinder person. I get to see life through my children's developing minds, which wonder at tiny ants crawling on the sidewalk or ponder larger things, such as the Big Bang, or questions like "why have we always lived on earth?" I am astounded by the questions a not-even-four-year-old can ask, and how much they ask and learn constantly. I want to teach them to think for themselves, to work hard, and to leave the world better place.

I am amazed by the love and devotion that small children have for their parents (and vice versa!) and other caregivers, and also by how much they depend on us to know the world and understand what it is to be part of humankind. I desire to make the world a better place through them: to teach them to love their friends (and enemies), to be objective, to learn, to teach, to give when they can, to be honest, and, when they are older, to work together to make the world a better place. My friends also amaze me through their kindness, generosity, and love of life. Our lives would certainly be poorer without them. My joy comes from the people around us, and being able to observe and enjoy the world together with them.

Photo: Tradewell with her daughter Daphne

MASSIMO PIGLIUCCI
PROFESSOR OF PHILOSOPHY
CITY UNIVERSITY OF NEW YORK
NEW YORK, NEW YORK

[INTERVIEW] What gives my life joy and meaning? My friends, my family, the fact that I'm healthy and I can enjoy the things that I like in life, my profession. I'm lucky enough to actually have one of those jobs where you can do pretty much whatever you want, nobody's setting your priorities. It's the kind of job where you get up on Monday morning and you can't wait to get to work. I'm paid to spend most of my life teaching, reading and writing, which are the three things that I like the most.

Meaning is constructed, and it's local. It has a lot to do with your relations. I have a small number of close friends that I see on a regular basis. Aristotle and Epicurus would tell you that if you have a small number of friends, you cannot have a large number of them, by definition. Not if by "friends" we mean somebody with whom you spend a lot of time and you're close to. You can have 1,000 "friends" on Facebook, in fact I understand that 1,000 is a small number over there, but those cannot actually be friends in the true sense of the word. They are people with whom you have some kind of relationship, which is fine, but that's different.

Human beings, unlike most or all other animals, are conscious of the fact that they're finite beings, and that they are going to die. We have to face the prospect of annihilation of our consciousness. And that's not a good prospect, if you love life. As Woody Allen famously put it, "I don't want to be immortal through my work, I want to be immortal through not dying."

But it's certainly got to be harder for an atheist at the end of his life, since he knows he's not going anywhere else. But there are pretty good secular role models to lead the way. My favorite is the philosopher David Hume. Besides the fact that he has been one of the most influential thinkers in my own intellectual formation, if you read his biography you'll find that the guy was incredibly calm and almost cheerful in the last months of his life. He knew he was going to die, but he had had a good life, he had enjoyed it and had done what he wanted to do. In fact, there were a number of religious neighbors who kept visiting him, waiting for the great infidel to finally see the light, change his mind and face up to God. But they were constantly disappointed, because he just went on to say, "It's okay, this is the end, and it's okay." So what are you going to do about death? Not much, and that's okay.

Photo: Pigliucci with Aristotle and Descartes

SHELLEY SEGAL
SINGER-SONGWRITER
MELBOURNE, AUSTRALIA

I was lucky to grow up in a musical environment. My father performed in a function band, mostly at weddings and Bar Mitzvahs. I remember doing my homework after school at the band's rehearsals, occasionally getting up to sing a song. At eleven I began singing with the band at various functions. Performing became a huge outlet for me, developing my confidence and sense of self-expression. I also learned how music could be a gift to others; it could enhance people's experiences in powerful ways.

Playing for over 15 years at people's celebrations has given my life so much joy and meaning. I consider it a privilege to be a part of significant events in others' lives. I also write and perform my own music, which has taken me all over the world. I am so grateful for the opportunity to travel, to share my reflections and to connect with people in this unique way.

My music has allowed me to grow on my own but also through meaningful collaborations. I have learned so much from the talented people that I have worked with. It is *electric* to be completely in the present moment, pushing yourself, surrounded by people who are working together, passionate about the same thing as you.

One of my greatest pleasures is playing music with my dad, who is my best friend. We are fortunate to have the opportunity to give back some of the joy that we have received through music. We play together at old folks homes. Dad will often accompany me when I play for The Sweet Princess Charitable Trust providing live music in the homes of sick children.

I have also had the privilege of teaching music, mostly to young people. It is so great to be able to pass on something that has given so much

meaning to my life. What a thrill to see kids get excited about something new that they have learned or a milestone they have reached. It makes me feel like I am a link in the chain of music and knowledge.

In my spare time I love to read. It is inspiring to consider that there is more to read and more to learn then I could ever manage in my whole life. There is never an excuse to be bored.

Spending time with my loved ones, family and friends brings a deep meaning to my life. It is my relationships with others that makes me feel as though my life has a purpose, that it matters.

Apocalyptic Love Song (For Hitchens)

One day the sun is going to die
For us it means no more sunsets
To the universe, just one less star in the sky

Almost all who ever lived, have already died
Countless stories of love and war and hope and pain
Now silent lay side by side

And yes I understand that my whole life is just a blink of an eye
In the history of the earth, as with each moment that goes by

But this moment that I'm with you
It feels like time has stood still
It feels somehow like it matters
And that it always will

In one billion years, the oceans will dry
While somehow life may continue
It will not be known to you and I

To think we are so important, is an obvious crime
We know that we are specks on a tiny dot
Hurtling through space and time

And yes I understand that my whole life is just a blink of an eye
In the history of the earth, as with each moment that goes by

But this moment that I'm with you
It feels like time has stood still
It feels somehow like it matters
And that it always will

JIM AL-KHALILI
PROFESSOR OF PHYSICS / AUTHOR / BROADCASTER
PORTSMOUTH, UNITED KINGDOM

[INTERVIEW] A lot of physicists like to quote that Richard Feynman piece where he says, "I have a friend who's an artist. He'll hold up a flower and say 'I as an artist can see how beautiful this is, but you as a scientist take this all apart and it becomes a dull thing,'" and Feynman says, "In fact I see the beauty that you see and more because I understand the laws of nature, and there's a beauty in the laws of nature." So what gives me joy is the fact that the Universe is comprehensible, that the laws governing it are logical—everything we learn about the laws of physics makes sense. And where there are still mysteries out there, they're only mysteries because we've yet to figure something out. It's that wonder in the laws of nature, I think, that gives me most joy.

I believe strongly—and this is down to my scientific training—that my atoms and molecules have come together to make me, me, by some incredible, wonderful accident. If you trace back all those links in the chain that had to be in place for me to be here, the laws of probability maintain that my very existence is miraculous. But then, after however many decades, less than a hundred years, they disburse and I cease to be. So while they're all congregated and coordinated to make me, then—and I speak here on behalf of all those trillions of atoms—I should really make the most of things.

So what inspires me? Well, I'm inspired by how nature does things in a way that should be logical, should make sense, but maybe doesn't always make sense to us. Those scientists who have made the big breakthroughs inspire me: how did they come to that conclusion based on the knowledge that was around at the time? How did they make that leap? Because they were right.

I'm also inspired by my wife, Julie, who's not a scientist and doesn't have a scientific training. But we've been together since we were 18, and we've been married for 26 years, so she's very much my soul mate and behind what I've been able to do with my life. She's enabled me to achieve what I have in my scientific career, and so I feel grateful she is happy because she's making me happy, allowing me to do what I do. I often ask her, "Are you sure you don't mind?" The thing is, she's not ambitious like me, she doesn't feel she needs to achieve, but just her support is a big inspiration for me.

CHANTAL P. YACAVONE
SOAPER / SMALL BUSINESS OWNER, *GREAT KARMA*
KALISPELL, MONTANA

I really believe that if I show my children they are accepted and loved and free to pursue their own course for happiness they will experience success on their own terms, free from judgment (mine and the world's).

Many people think atheism means that we live in opposition to the worship of Yahweh or the God of Abraham, and as a consequence they have it stuck in their heads that we don't value life or that death doesn't mean anything to us. Nothing could be further from the truth. In fact, it is really the complete opposite. Life, because it is so fleeting and precious, means everything to us. Being a nontheist actually makes finding joy and purpose much easier. We know that life could be gone in a moment, so we try to wring out of it every moment of happiness that we possibly can. One of the little things that brings me happiness is the fact that for the past 20 years whenever my husband leaves the house he kisses me goodbye and says, "Drive safe, honey, I love you." I, in turn, can't send my children off for the day without kissing them goodbye, sometimes too many times. It's a bit superstitious, but when you know in your heart that there is nothing but the here and now, it becomes vitally important to live for today. I want my children to go out into the world each time feeling loved, accepted, and like they have a safe place within their family whenever they need it.

My husband and I try to maintain a haven for our children within the family unit, even when everything seems chaotic and one or all of us

is hurting. For example, last year during spring break we took a trip that had been planned for months. My father-in-law had been ill for many years, and my husband had been to visit his parents just two weeks prior to help move his father into hospice and finalize some details with his mother. The first day of our trip we got the call that his father had passed away. Rob and his mother made arrangements for the funeral service to be held after we returned home, but we still had a week to spend in this lovely tropical location while we were all feeling terribly sad and brokenhearted. Rather than return to our normal routine and ignore our pain as we might have done at home, we had this uninterrupted week together as a family where life was slow and easy, and we ate every meal together without any outside distractions. It allowed us time to reconnect, reflect, and reset without the outside world intruding. By the end of the week, we all agreed that despite the circumstances, it was the best family vacation we had ever been on.

Despite differing approaches, my husband and I were both raised with love. It is a gift to be able to pass that love from one generation to the next. At the end of our time on this earth, if our own children are able to say that we raised them with love and understanding, we will have succeeded as parents. To us, raising our children to think for themselves and to find their own happiness brings us, as parents, all the joy and meaning life has to offer.

Photo: Yacavone with her family (left to right): daughter Pascale, son Garrett, husband Rob, and son Tony (son Vincent not pictured)

ANDREW COPSON
CHIEF EXECUTIVE, BRITISH HUMANIST ASSOCIATION
LONDON, UNITED KINGDOM

[INTERVIEW] The idea of joy in life is a really interesting idea. Obviously, we all have periods of intense happiness, which we can sometimes recognize, but more often recognize retrospectively after they're over. The times in my life at which I felt this sort of high sense of joy, of extreme happiness, have been ones mostly connected with other people. I can think of moments spent with my grandmother as a child. I can think of moments spent with people that I've loved in my adult life, romantically but also as friends. The first time that one of my godchildren—we have to call them godchildren in English because there's no equivalent secular word, unlike in French, so we struggle with the word godchildren—anyway, I have three of them, and I remember when one of them fell asleep in my arms and I felt a great lance of joy inside. Heightened feelings like that have mostly come to me through other people.

I've also attained those sorts of feelings at particular points of engagement with culture, particular moments in stories I've read or TV programs I've watched where some incident, often involving a quite rich characterization of people coming together at a particular time, has taken me with it, sort of lifted me up with the narrative of it, the flow of the story.

But then there's another meaning of joy, I think, which is a continued feeling of contentment and happiness that goes on and on rather than just the sort of pinpoints of experience that you might feel at the time and then recall. I've been happiest over a long period of time in my work. I'm very, very lucky to be amongst a very small minority— not just of people today, but of people who've ever lived—to have work that I love, that I find to be meaningful in itself and for what it achieves. To run a humanist organization is to adopt some very worthwhile goals in relation to public policy, to improving the lives of others, and to connecting with other people and wider society. The pursuing of those goals over time has given me the most settled and continuous feeling of meaning, fulfillment and happiness that I've had.

CHARLES STROUSE
BROADWAY COMPOSER (*ANNIE, BYE BYE BIRDIE*)
NEW YORK, NEW YORK

[INTERVIEW] I'm 84 and I'm feeling great. I have my good days and bad like anyone else. I think one of the most inspiring things to me is if I compose something I think is felicitous, technically competent. My family inspires me to do better. I love my wife. The business of inspiration to most creators and artists is a very confusing one because mostly in my experience the act of composing or painting, comes not from inspiration but from working at it. It's a technical thing that brings wonderful fruits of your labor if you do it consistently and well. So it's a tough topic to talk about without being very flowery about it. I mean, I like a beautiful sky and the smell of flowers as much as the next person. But I've always been inspired by the fact that I went from this note to that note, and somehow in between made a line— or a note in conjunction with another note—that gave me interest and pleasure. After that it's all up to fate or whatever you want to call it being an atheist. I can't call it God. It's all up to the musicians who perform it and the audiences who hear it and the critics who criticize it. In my own heart I try and do the best I can.

The idea of an afterlife seems rather ridiculous to me. I've had surgery and survived it, having fainted and been unconscious and come to, and experienced all of the systems of your body closing off. You're not sleeping, you're without consciousness. Now I know some people have reported after coming from that, they've seen bright lights and angels and all kinds of things. I don't know. You know, I think given the world we live in, you're almost tempted to say anything is possible. But that said, I don't believe that anything will happen except all my systems will close off and I just hope it's not painful.

I'm terribly attached to my children and my wife. There are so many things that have given me pleasure and, being very sensitive to the winds of fortune, a lot of things that have given me sadness. Even things that religious people have said to me. You know, for instance, the failure of a work of mine or disdain of a critic, that's given me great unhappiness. And many people have said to me if I believed in God, he would be whispering in my ear and, well...that has not happened to me. I've been despondent and I've been elated. The two don't seem to hold although somebody who is religious might say, "Ah, but you haven't tried it." Indeed I've had some religious friends who say God is your friend and if you carry him, if you believe in him, he'll be whispering in your ear. It hasn't happened to me.

"The sun'll come out..."

In the musical *Annie*, what Martin Charnin (who wrote the lyrics) and I had mind with the song "Tomorrow," was that there are certain things that are sure and regular like the sun coming up—the rain falling, the clouds sailing, etc. There's that regularity of life, I think, that influences any living being. Why clouds keep forming in the sky or birds developed out of dinosaurs or grass grows and faces the sun? Those are questions I don't know much about. But my belief is that those things do not come from a bearded man in the sky.

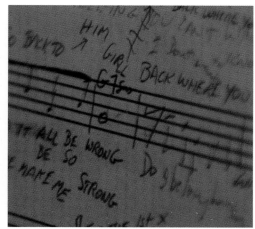

DAVID NIOSE
ATTORNEY / AUTHOR / PRESIDENT, SECULAR COALITION FOR AMERICA
FITCHBURG, MASSACHUSETTS

[INTERVIEW] Humanism is an affirmative worldview and it's much more than just nonbelief. Though atheism is a term that also accurately describes me—I'm an atheist because I don't believe in divinities. The word "atheist" has been scorned for too long in America, and that has empowered religious conservatives, so those of us who don't believe should help change that by accepting the label openly, by not running from it. But humanist is an entire naturalistic worldview—it's an affirmative set of values, a standard of ethics, and an acceptance of science and empiricism. It accurately describes who I am, beyond my atheism.

The same things that give joy and meaning to most people give joy and meaning to me—my family, my friends, people I love, people I respect, doing things that interest me. I'm interested in politics and public policy and social issues and activism, and that's what I roll up my sleeves and get into on a day-to-day basis, and I just enjoy it. It gives me meaning and I do it without any belief in

divinities. Frankly, I think a lot of people, even many who happen to have God-belief, find their joy and meaning through real-world activities, not through believing in deities.

I really think humanism and the emergence of America's seculars is the cause of our age. Back in the beginning of the twentieth century, W.E.B. Du Bois looked forward and predicted the issue of that century was going to be the issue of race, and if you think about that, he was right. He was standing only a generation removed from the Civil War, Jim Crow was still way out of hand, there was segregation, and so forth. Looking out at American culture at that point in time, you'd have to say that this country had to get its act together on race. Now, a hundred years later, I'm not suggesting the issue of race is behind us, but certainly we've come a long way. There is still economic injustice and social injustice, but we've elected an African-American president, here in Massachusetts we've elected an African-American governor, interracial relationships are

commonplace and accepted, and I think we've made some real progress, and I would hope that race is not going to be the big issue of the twenty-first century.

What is going to be the big issue of this century? I would suggest that, with fundamentalist Christians exerting enormous influence in American public life and the secular demographic totally marginalized in American politics, you'd have to say the question of fundamentalist religion and the secular demographic's emergence is the issue of the century. I mean, it's assumed that if you're an open atheist, you're not a viable candidate for any public office. A hundred years from now, if America is still in the position it is now—with fundamentalist Christians wielding great power and seculars marginalized—I shudder to think what this country and this world will look like. If we ever want to see rational, sane, people-oriented public policy, we need an emergence of the secular demographic.

RUSSELL GLASSER
SOFTWARE ENGINEER
CO-HOST, *THE ATHEIST EXPERIENCE*
AUSTIN, TEXAS

I love to listen to contrary opinions, and it was while listening to Christian radio one day that I heard a pop psychology claim that all atheists are motivated by hatred of their fathers. It was probably the funniest thing I ever heard, because my love for my family is a big part of what has shaped me as an outspoken proponent of freethought.

I'm a fourth generation atheist—my parents both have PhD's in physics, are both non-believers from Jewish families, and they named me after Bertrand Russell. My father, a computational plasma physicist, had been an atheist all his life. I was probably set on a path to being an atheist activist around the time I went to kindergarten in Auburn, Alabama, when most of my peers couldn't even get their minds around the idea that it was possible to live without believing in God. I had to consult with my dad because I had no idea how to answer questions from competing six-year-olds, such as, "Who created the world then?"

His father, a dentist from New York, was also a lifelong atheist. And his father, according to family lore, died peacefully of old age while reading Bertrand Russell in bed. My son, while still pretty young and working to shape his own philosophy of life, has given every indication that he'll be carrying on the family tradition as a fifth generation atheist.

I happened to be an undergraduate student just as the Internet was starting to dramatically redefine the way human interactions are handled on a worldwide scale. Email and social networks have been a huge factor in creating an interconnected atheist movement. Much like a kindergartner in the Deep South, most atheists don't have a lot of friends and mentors with similar views, and they can often feel isolated and conflicted. Being able to tap into a network full of scientists and philosophers and entertainers who share their views has been a huge gift to atheists feeling the need for support.

I enjoy arguing, and, after being on my high school debate team, I was incredibly lucky to cross paths with the crew of *The Atheist Experience*. Back then it was a promising public access show and today it is very successful online series with a global audience. I want to reach out to fellow skeptics everywhere and let them know that they're not alone, that they hold an intellectually satisfying position, and that loving life isn't dependent on believing faith-based stories.

LYNNEA GLASSER
GAME DEVELOPER
CO-HOST, *GODLESS BITCHES* PODCAST
AUSTIN, TEXAS

I have made it my life's goal to spend as much time as possible creating positive experiences for others, and cultivating an atmosphere for future generations to be able to enjoy themselves as well. I find my joy in justice and equality: in all creatures having opportunities for enjoyment and being treated with fairness, as we all wish and deserve to be treated. I promote social justice, empathy, and empowerment, because that is what all thinking beings deserve during their lifetime. I fight for this in my mortal life, because I know that there is no afterlife and therefore no posthumous reward or punishment. I know that the only justice in the world is the justice we create ourselves, and so I strive to make this world as fair and positive as possible for as many people as I can. I am most elated when others around me are happy, healthy, and treated fairly.

I also get some of my joy from a sense of personal accomplishment: I work hard at my job, write videogames, keep an orderly house, cook, watch movies, and ride bikes. But while I enjoy the positive feelings of self-improvement, this fire pales compared to the feeling of joy that comes from having contributed something to the greater good—something that will serve and be enjoyed by others. This is why I got involved with the Atheist Community of Austin, the *Godless Bitches* podcast, the *Non-Prophets* podcast, and even once with *The Atheist Experience* TV show. I've written blog posts with an emphasis on life improvement, I worked to save the environment, I protested the war, I boycotted bigoted or corrupt businesses, I volunteered with the National Domestic Violence Hotline, and I know that the work I've done to improve the world has just begun.

I live content knowing that the efforts I've made towards creating a more secular and rational society—a better society—has reached and helped others, and that they in turn will be in a better position to reach out and help others themselves. It is additive. Mortal life is an unyielding, unwinnable battle against entropy, apathy, and malaise that can only be kept at bay if we work together in determined positivity. At least once a week, I hold my husband, Russell Glasser, close to me as he sleeps and mourn for the day when he will be gone. I live happily, enjoying what little time we two have had together. Even though I know what we have is fleeting, I can only hold onto what we do have, and love and cherish that. I am content hoping that we will continue to improve the human condition, and I the dream that perhaps one day we can eliminate death and suffering altogether here on Earth.

A. C. GRAYLING

PHILOSOPHER / AUTHOR / MASTER OF THE NEW COLLEGE OF THE HUMANITIES
LONDON, UNITED KINGDOM

[INTERVIEW] When I was quite young I lived in Africa, and the African sky at night is unpolluted by light. When you look up into the heavens of the Southern Hemisphere you see a brilliant array of stars. It really looks as if that black velvet background is studded with jewelry, scintillating away. I always used to be amazed at the great clarity of the night sky, too, meaning that when the moon was full, you could see detail on it with the naked eye. So that sense of being in a place as vast as the continent of Africa with all its wildlife, and that great sky above us, that great ceiling so brilliantly lit up, was an early experience. You could read by the starlight. That was always a source of wonder.

And the world has continued to be a source of wonder ever since, because it doesn't have to be the Grand Canyon, it could be a city street, it could be the face of another human being. Everything is full of wonder.

I'm fond of repeating (at every possible opportunity) what Solon the Athenian lawgiver said to King Croesus. He said you've got to remember that a human life is less than a thousand months long. Do the math: supposing you live until you're 80, what's 12 times 80? It's less than a thousand months. Now a third of them, three hundred months, you're asleep. Another third of them, you're waiting in line somewhere, at Duane Reade, say.

So you have about three hundred months to live with passion and vividness, to live trying to do something, make something, trying to create some significance in your own life and the lives of people you care about, and indeed the world in general. And that's quite a challenge, but it's a good challenge. And so it means that one must not waste time. As the cobblers used to say, work while you have light. So while you're here, while you have your three hundred months, you must put all your energy into it.

I think it's our responsibility to make meaning in life. It's quite a difficult one, because most people are anxious about whether they can really think things through. It takes a lot of reading and discussing and learning and thinking to try to make a bit of progress on that front. But that's what it is to be human. We have this wonderful capacity for reflection, we have intelligence and we should use it.

So when theists say, "Oh you're missing something," I say one of the things we're missing is what has caused so much division and conflict and oppression in human history. I think about the history of gays, for example, and women, most especially, all of whom have been badly served by religion in the past. And so I think it's a wonderful thing to liberate the human mind from all these ancient traditions of thought, and allow each individual to see the world fresh, and to decide for themselves how they're going to live in it.

The world is such a fascinating place. And the great endeavor of humankind is to try to ameliorate its own condition, to try to help those who are struggling, to educate ourselves, to inquire more into the nature of the world, to put to work the knowledge that we get. And to make the very best that we can of our capacity to enjoy things like natural beauty, art, and literature. To tell one another stories about what it is to be human. All these things are full of elements that can be celebrated. And which, when we embrace them, make life very, very rich.

DON YONKER
MUSICIAN / PRODUCER
PEDERICKTOWN, NEW JERSEY

I've been a punk rocker since 1985. Hearing the first ten seconds of Black Flag's "Rise Above" transformed me. Prior to that I'd been exposed to some punk music but nothing had grabbed me by the collar and shaken me like that song. Ironically, born-again Christians are most likely to relate to such a moment. The main difference being that my epiphany led me to challenge authority and dogma instead of being seduced by them. Ultimately, it's what led me to atheism. Thinking for one's self and demanding proof are part and parcel of the punk ethos and to this day those values have served me well.

It turns out that my transformation wasn't unique and there was an entire community of skeptical malcontents awaiting me. It was a volatile, exciting, and demanding community but also an accepting and empowering one. Misfits of most stripes were welcome. Healthy skepticism and spiky hair bonded us and seeing a complete stranger with Dr. Martens boots or purple hair meant that within minutes your stranger status would end. Instant friendships were made and our world consisted of "us" and "them." Being one of "them," the tract home-dwelling, khakis-wearing, flavorless drones whose legions seemed endless would have been existential death. Living our lives on our own terms gave them meaning. Avoiding what Thoreau called "lives of quiet desperation" was paramount.

Connecting with other people who shared this worldview was deeply important to me and I'm not sure what would have become of me had I not felt the camaraderie of the punk scene. It taught me that the world doesn't have to be "every man for himself." It taught me that others matter. My fellow punks mattered to me and I mattered to them. What didn't matter was convention. In our scene, building your life without the stifling conventions of modern society earned respect and provided a sense of accomplishment. I think feeling a sense of accomplishment, whether from building a model airplane, winning a race, or scoring an A in math brings joy to people's lives. Accomplishing goals bolsters our self-worth, gives us confidence, and makes us eager to take on new challenges. To the punks of my generation, every day lived on our terms brought a sense of accomplishment. Our existence alone was a triumph over convention and every day was meaningful.

Being a musician in this atmosphere has led to truly sublime moments for me. Wailing on a Les Paul guitar while hundreds of like-minded misfits slam-dance and pogo-dance and generally lose their minds creates an energy and connection that most people never get to experience. The best part is that in those moments I'm sure the audience feels it the way I do. In those moments there is an energy that is shared between me, my band mates, and the audience that I've yet to feel anywhere else. Some people say they have the same feeling in churches. I don't need churches for my transcendent moments. I need dirty punk-rock clubs.

Photos: Yonker performing with his band, Tonight We Strike, in Brooklyn, New York

JANET ASIMOV
PSYCHIATRIST / AUTHOR
NEW YORK, NEW YORK

Although I've been a disbeliever since high school, I tended to be inhibited about offending believers (like some ultraconservative and fortunately distant relatives). After meeting Isaac, I was impressed by his matter-of-fact admission of his own atheism, acknowledging it in print and on television.

Being able to say one does not believe in the supernatural is liberating. And now we can smile when scolded by those who say we must lead unhappy lives. Research has shown that atheists are not as depressed as believers, who are trapped in their need to have "happily ever after" be true.

Well, it isn't. Happily is possible now and then. I admit that I was a lot happier with Isaac than I have been as a widow, but loss does not make me long for "ever after." I think one reason believers have hidden depression is that in the effort to ensure that they and their loved ones live forever, they don't really live in the present. They worry about past sins and future punishments or rewards. They even louse up the environment because only heaven matters.

Isaac wanted not only to entertain people but to help them learn about and experience what he loved in science. There is joy in the search for knowledge about the universe in all its manifestations, including human beings, but it's necessary to accept uncertainty (we don't and can't know it all) or we're off and running to some omniscient parent figure who promises that we can have forever after, with no pain in endings.

Human life, like the universe itself, has a beginning, a middle, and an end—much as a good story does. When Isaac was dying, he didn't expect or ask for a permanent and personal hereafter. But he did hope that a few of his books would be read in the future. All writers hope that.

Creativity doesn't make permanence certain, but it does make life joyous and fulfilling. Isaac and I were lucky to have known that. Since there are many ways of being creative and helpful to others (like being a great cook), my hope is that everyone can find that way of living life happily, if not ever after.

SEAN CARROLL

THEORETICAL PHYSICIST, CALIFORNIA INSTITUTE OF TECHNOLOGY
LOS ANGELES, CALIFORNIA

[INTERVIEW] Many things give my life joy and meaning. The first obvious clichéd but true thing is that I'm married. I have the best wife in the world, Jennifer, another atheist/agnostic. And we have fun. We're explorers and experimenters, we try to do different things. We both write books. I try to figure out how the world works and then I try to communicate whatever it is we figured out to other people. Just the idea that we, these little collections of atoms and molecules, are part of the world, but a part that can look at the rest of the world and figure it out in a self-referential way, is kind of breathtaking. That would be the big abstract way of thinking about joy and meaning. What I actually like is good food and good drinks and playing poker, watching movies and reading books, listening to music and having a good time. Being a good person, helping others learn about this amazing universe we live in.

The universe isn't tuned to my wishes, of course. There are aspects I would change. I'd like to live a long time if I were given the option. And I suspect science is going to give us the option someday but probably not until it's too late for me. It adds a certain spice to life knowing you have only a certain amount of time. Our lives are performances, not dress rehearsals. Neither the universe, nor any external supernatural beings, tell us what to do or provide us with explicit goals, but we have the ability to create such goals for ourselves. This—what we have and what we are doing right here and right now—this is what matters. You can't help but be moved by the significance of that.

So I have a very good life. My life is full of joy and happiness and meaning, so I have no desire whatsoever to have it end. There are many places I want to go and things I want to do. But I accept that it ends and I truly feel that that acceptance makes it much easier for me to deal with death than for people who don't quite understand what will happen.

How we think about death determines to a large extent how we think about life, and your attitude toward reality plays a big part in that. My belief is that when somebody dies they're no longer here anymore. That will include me, someday. The people who are here continue to matter, and when people die, their memory lives on in other people.

Every physicist or mathematician knows that there's many wrong ways to get a right answer. It's very possible to lead a joyful, meaningful life without understanding correctly the fundamental workings of the universe. But the chances are better that you're going to reach those goals correctly if you do have the right understanding. I'm lucky enough to have a job that involves figuring out some of the most profound aspects of how reality works. I was there in Geneva when they announced the Higgs Boson was discovered. The big reveal is when they show a little plot with some dots on it. If you didn't know the context, you wouldn't really know what it meant. It was a little bump and they even draw a line through the dots to emphasize it because you wouldn't be able to notice the bump otherwise. Because I've studied something about the workings of the physical universe, I understand that this bump represents an idea that people had in the 1960s. Given what we knew about the weak interactions of particle physics back then, we knew there must be a certain kind of particle and we would spend decades and billions of dollars, and thousands of people would devote their energies to finding it. And there's this little bump $9 billion later. The fact that it's there is awesome, but also the fact that human beings—just by thinking about it, by thinking about how we could fit the constraints that the data gave us—were able in the 1960s to project ahead over 40 years and say there we would find this little bump in the data someday. The ability of human beings to figure out the world never ceases to amaze me. I've been lucky enough to sort of be a very, very tiny part of that in a very minor way, which is a great privilege for me.

Nevertheless, much of my joy and meaning comes from the same places everybody else gets them from. Falling in love. Having a long day and sitting down at the end of it with a glass of wine and some cheese and talking to my wife. Watching a good TV show or reading something interesting. Having fun. Learning about the world, helping others learn about it, giving something back. In a way, it's sad to imagine that some people can't find true happiness or meaning without relying on a kind of supernatural justification. We are just collections of atoms, obeying the laws of physics. But we are self-reflective collections of atoms, with the ability to contemplate ourselves and our universe. We have the ability to find meaning, and even better, to create meaning along the way. It's a wonderful opportunity as well as an intimidating responsibility. I don't get to choose how the world is, but given that this is the world in which we find ourselves, I'm certainly going to make the most of it.

MARYAM NAMAZIE
CAMPAIGNER
LONDON, UNITED KINGDOM

Islamists want atheists dead. Under Sharia law, apostasy is punishable in over 20 countries; blasphemy in over 30. Even in Europe, ex-Muslim atheists are often not free to reveal that they have renounced Islam, due to not wanting to disappoint their families, fear of being ostracized or threats and intimidation.

Despite this, multiculturalism (not as a positive lived experience but as a segregationist social policy) ignores and negates the plight of ex-Muslims, giving precedence to cultures and religion rather than people and their rights and lives. And it says that human beings—depending on how they are pigeon-holed—are fundamentally different, and should be treated as such. This point of view sees Islamist values and sensibilities as that of "authentic Muslims," thereby shrinking secular spaces and making dissent ever more difficult and often life-threatening.

Effectively, therefore, concepts such as rights, equality, respect and tolerance, which were initially raised vis-à-vis the individual, are now applied more and more to culture and religion and often take precedence over real live human beings. Moreover, the social inclusion of people into society has come to solely mean the inclusion of their beliefs, sensibilities, concerns and agendas (read Islamism's beliefs, sensibilities, concerns and agendas) and nothing more.

Though Muslims or those labeled as such are Islamism's first victims and on the frontlines of resistance, the conflation of Islam and Islamism with Muslims has meant that much needed criticism is often condemned as racism. Rather, the idea of difference has always been the fundamental principle of a racist agenda, not the other way around.

The distinction between humans and their beliefs and far-right political movements is of crucial significance here.

It is the human being who is meant to be equal, not his or her beliefs. It is the human being who is worthy of the highest respect and rights, not his or her beliefs or those imputed on them.

It is the human being who is sacred, not beliefs or religion.

Religion sees things the other way around. And when in power will stop at nothing to prove it.

And this is the main reason why religion must be relegated to the private sphere. More importantly than the fact that it divides, excludes, denies, restricts and kills is the compelling fact that when it comes to religion, it is not the equality, rights, freedoms, welfare of the child, man or woman that is paramount, but religious dogma itself.

In the face of Islamism, the right to criticize and break the taboo that comes with renouncing Islam are historical tasks.

This is why we must call ourselves ex-Muslims, even though other atheists don't call themselves ex-Christian or ex-Jewish. We must because we can still be killed for leaving Islam. Under such dire circumstances, using the very term ex-Muslim is an important form of resistance and dissent.

Islamists want us to submit to Allah's will? I don't think so. We will shout out our atheism and our renunciation of Islam from every rooftop.

This, of course, may not sound very joyful but there is a lot of joy in refusing and resisting. Yes, it's difficult and can be painful but it still feels pretty good (even on a bad day).

TROY BOYLE

CORPORATE PARALEGAL / LAW STUDENT / COMIC BOOK ARTIST / FOUNDER, NATIONAL ATHEIST PARTY
CRITTENDEN, KENTUCKY

I discovered atheism by accident. Unhappy with the religious institutions that I'd been introduced to (Catholicism, Southern Baptist, and Episcopalianism), I asked myself a simple question at 12 years old: What is the Truth? The capital "T" Truth? The objective, infinite, always-true truth that isn't situational or dependent upon the circumstances of one's birth.

I began reading. *Bullfinch's Mythology* (1881) and *Mythology* by Edith Hamilton (1942). What did other cultures believe? Rather than dismissing ancient stories as myth and legend, what beliefs did these people live and die by? We think of Odinism, for instance, as quaint heroic legends that inspired at least one successful comic book series, but it's important to realize—and it was the focus of my pre-teen inquiry—that these stories, now regarded as distant and naive myths and parables, were the daily worship of these people. Not just the Vikings and Germanic peoples, but the Celts and the ancient Egyptians, Romans, Native Americans and others. They *believed* in their gods and goddesses, heroes and antagonists. They died with their names on their lips. From Norway to Tenochtitlan, a panoply of hundreds of pre-Christian deities were worshipped, sacrificed to, prayed to, loved, trusted and ultimately abandoned as these cultures changed, matured or died out.

The lessons I learned from this deep foray into the human mytho-poetic experience are many and have lasted a lifetime. They call out in their similarity of structure and narrative to a longing need by humanity for understanding and self-worth. The hierarchical arrangements of their gods and heroes reflect the social arrangements and division of political power in their respective societies, and as such, they are valuable and entertaining material. I *love* reading and discovery and the transcendent experience of allowing another mind to guide mine into realms unimagined. This is the power of books and reading.

I came to understand that religion is politics and power; stories and narratives, all intended to make an incomprehensible universe and life manageable. I look back on it fondly but it is no longer necessary. Psychology, social ethics, community, science and education have replaced every function that religion once had, and have more accurately explained every phenomenon that religion attempted to relegate to the gods. I discovered, in short, that religion is obsolete.

But you cannot feed the mind and starve the body and attempt to remain whole. When I'm not reading or writing you can find me on any of the various sixteen Frisbee golf courses in Greater Cincinnati. I love the sport and the pastime. It gets me outside, provides a moderate cardiovascular workout and bragging rights if any of my kids or friends are keen to step up and challenge me. I recommend Frisbee golf (or disc golf, as it is more snobbily known) to anyone of any age or fitness level that wants to get outside for a couple of hours and enjoy a pastoral hobby in the great outdoors. If you haven't tried it before, you'll thank me for the rest of your life—which I hope is a long and prosperous one. Cheers.

LAURA COOPER
BIRTH DOULA
TORONTO, ONTARIO, CANADA

I was raised Catholic and attended church with my family every Sunday until about the age of 16. My religious beliefs were steadily eroded as I moved away from my family, went to university, learned more about the world, and met a variety of people. I realize that I had experienced many of the teachings of the Catholic church as harmful. These teachings and practices included the use of fear, shame, reward, and threat of punishment to control thoughts and behavior; the emphasis on faith and rigidly prescribed morality over questioning and critical thinking; the devaluing of life on earth and the present moment by shifting the gaze heavenward; the belief that women are inferior and subservient to men; the secrecy, shame, and misinformation surrounding sexuality; the labeling of people with different beliefs as sinners, to be shunned or converted; and the list goes on. What all of these harmful beliefs have in common is that they are obstacles to or cheap substitutions for true autonomy, connection, and peak experience. Deconstructing the ways in which my religious upbringing has done harm has been very healing for me as I cultivate a sense of purpose and self as an atheist adult. It has also been empowering to know that there are parts of my evolved human nature that no amount of religious indoctrination could touch—I am a socially connected, cognitively flexible human being, and joy and meaning are within my grasp.

As a child, I encountered connection and peak experience through play, especially in nature. There was the winter in Juneau, Alaska when the lake froze so solidly in front of the Mendenhall Glacier that we could skate right up to its massive face. I was stunned, enveloped by the beauty of this huge wall of shining white and blue ice, jutting into the sky and trailing out into a huge sheet, so smooth, stretching for what seemed like miles, and rippling with reflected sunshine. There was a winter night when my mother got my sister and me all bundled up and drove us to Twin Lakes Park so the three of us could lay outstretched on the frozen lake, to watch the aurora borealis dance across the night sky. Soft snow dusted our faces as we shared an awed but peaceful silence. There were endless hours tearing through the trees and neighborhood streets with all the other sun-soaked children in summertime. We waded waist-deep into the waters of Jordan Creek to catch minnows in plastic buckets and dared each other to climb the evergreen trees that towered well above our neighbors' three-story house. We learned to do bold things safely; God wasn't holding us in some heavenly harness—we were testing our weight on each branch, experimenting, using our bodies, trusting our senses, and cooperating.

As an adult, connection and peak experience come from my work. I recently changed careers, from scientist to self-employed birth doula. I serve women by providing physical, emotional, and informational support as they prepare to give birth, as they labour, and in the early postpartum period. Building a trust relationship with each client is fundamental. Connections are built by cultivating empathy and by creating a safe space in which there is freedom to be vulnerable. I often have to dedicate a lot of time to dispelling myths and fears surrounding childbirth, as most of my clients come from a culture that is very fearful of the process. I wonder how much of this culture comes from the dominant religions, which feature elaborate systems of taboo, secrecy, and shaming to control women's sexuality and self-knowledge, which would otherwise be great sources of power, authenticity, and self-determination. Fear and shame also derail our ability to connect to others, so veiling female sexuality and reproductive abilities in secrecy keeps women from connecting.

One great antidote against fear is knowledge about the anatomy and physiology of labour and birth. My clients are often empowered in knowing that evolution has selected for female bodies well adapted to birthing, that they are not machines on the verge of imminent breakdown, nor are they victims in need of rescue. The pain of childbirth is not Eve's Curse. It is an integral part of the hormonal feedback system regulating everything from uterine contractions, to pushing the baby out, to bonding. Sharing this knowledge with my clients and encouraging them to do their own research not only helps them connect to their process and build their sense of autonomy, but also helps me connect to them. The learning process often brings relief, fascination, and joy.

In birth, a woman surrenders to something greater than herself; to the natural forces, to an ancient and evolved biology. Through this surrender, many women understand that labour is a crucible, not a crucifix. In surrendering, they find new strength, which will serve them well as mothers. Perhaps the most important support I give is in staying connected and present, adapting to the changing demands of the moment. The more I learn to do this for each woman, the more I realize that I am experiencing a tremendous gift: to observe and to experience a state of total loss of self-consciousness and sense of time; to hold a space where love unfolds and to be touched by it, without feeling I have to own the experience that is uniquely hers and her child's. I feel immense gratitude in being able to witness something at once so astonishing and so ordinary.

RICHARD DAWKINS
EVOLUTIONARY BIOLOGIST / AUTHOR
OXFORD, UNITED KINGDOM

The fact of our own existence is wonderfully strange. Even more wonderful and strange is the very fact that we are capable of understanding the process that gave rise to us. From simple beginnings—some physicists say literally from nothing—the processes of natural physics gave rise to matter and chemistry, and then the processes of natural biology gave rise to living things. Evolution by Darwinian natural selection gave rise to an astonishing diversity of animals, plants and micro-organisms—diverse, yet united in one task: the preservation and propagation of the DNA that built them. There's a delicious inevitability about the whole business. The world becomes filled with DNA that is good at making copies of itself, but exactly how it does it varies from the simplicity of a virus to the complexity of an elephant. Elephant DNA is like a computer program that says: "Make more copies of this program but do it by the roundabout route of building an elephant first. "

The brain is an evolved on-board computer that runs a different kind of program, but even the brain is ultimately working for the preservation of the DNA that built it. Most animals have brains, but the human brain is in a class of its own. It has evolved large size and versatility, leading to emergent properties: things that no longer obviously serve the purpose of propagating DNA—mathematics, music, philosophy, poetry. And the conscious awareness that our life will come to an end. Not believing in an afterlife

gives greater meaning and greater fullness to the one life we have. You don't mess around wasting your time in this life because you expect to have another one. You're not going to get another life. Make the most of this one.

Giving up religion doesn't mean giving up the sensibilities that religion sometimes claims to monopolize. *Desert Island Discs* is a BBC program in which a "castaway" on an imaginary desert island is invited to choose eight records to take. The idea is to spin a little story of your life around music. One of the records I chose was from Bach's "St. Matthew Passion," *Mache dich mein Herze rein*. It's about the passion of Christ. The presenter, who was evidently religious herself in a sort of weak way, obstinately refused to understand why I chose this religious piece. It showed remarkable shallowness of understanding on her part. Did she imagine that I couldn't enjoy a work of fiction because I know the characters in the novel aren't real? Of course an atheist can appreciate great music even though it is about the passion of Jesus. It's fiction and it's great fiction: it's great music. Bach is sublime, like Schubert, Beethoven, Mozart. Their works are consummate achievements of the human spirit. Shakespeare too, and who would be so blind, who would be so deaf as not to swell with pride at these pinnacles of the human species, supreme culminations of the evolutionary process?

DAVID SILVERMAN
PRESIDENT, AMERICAN ATHEISTS
CHAIR OF THE REASON RALLY
CRANFORD, NEW JERSEY

[INTERVIEW] What gives my life meaning is honesty and truth; honesty and truth defeat bigotry and hatred.

I'm the kind of activist who wears atheist shirts out in public, wearing my atheism on my sleeve, literally. Back in the 1990s, most of the shirt feedback I got was negative, but occasionally somebody would give me a thumbs-up or some other subtle sign of approval. The shirt helped give these closeted atheists some comfort; it made them realize that they were not alone. And sometimes people would actually start talking to me: "Listen, I'm one of you. I'm an atheist, too." "Thank you for wearing that shirt. That's a great shirt." And that gave me the charge.

Since that time, there has been a drastic change in responses. I still keep wearing my atheist shirts everywhere, but for several years now I have not gotten a single negative reaction, and that includes travel all through the Bible Belt. Instead I get compliments all the time, on a regular basis. On my last trip, four TSA agents positively mentioned my shirt in security. "Nice shirt." "I'm with you." "Where can I find out more about it?" "Where can I get that shirt?" That kind of stuff is happening all the time now.

Wearing my atheism on my sleeve over time has afforded me a perspective on America's acceptance of atheism that I would not otherwise have had. I'm seeing positive progress for atheists to be more comfortable with their own identity and to come out in their own society. They know they're not alone. They know there's no need to whisper. In fact, there's a need *not* to whisper, and that's getting out. And now we're looking at the polls and we're seeing the numbers getting better and better for atheists. Every poll shows an improvement for atheism and an increase in tolerance for atheists. We're making serious progress for equality based on truth and honesty, even politically incorrect truth and honesty. That's what gives me that charge.

PATRICIA S. CHURCHLAND

NEUROPHILOSOPHER, UNIVERSITY OF CALIFORNIA SAN DIEGO
SAN DIEGO, CALIFORNIA

[INTERVIEW] What gives my life joy and meaning is what has given meaning to humans always and probably gave meaning to many species of hominin. And the story is neither very original nor very glamorous. No bizarre rituals or ugsome sacrifices or uncomfortable costumes are at its core.

Life's meaning depends on having close attachments—family, friends and those we love. Meaning also derives from having work or some skill you can take pride in. For different people, different kinds of work are satisfying and a source of significance. The work can be quite menial but still be something in which you take great deal of pride and satisfaction. Additionally, many of those wonderful but humdrum, day-to-day things that matter are part of happiness and meaning. This morning I was walking the dogs on the golf course and the remnants of the storm last night were visible. The clouds were moving in a remarkable way and the sun was coming up, and the light had this very spectacular, but transient quality to it. We respond positively to beauty, we find beauty in unpredictable places and times—if we are open to it. What else? Play is important. Not just as children but as we grow up. So part of the reason that I enjoy the dogs is they're so much fun to play with. Play adds the joy and lightness to life. It is good for the brain, as it down-regulates stress hormones. Connection to the wider community is also essential, and being engaged, in some way for the good of the community, whatever that community, is a factor in a meaningful life. We long to belong, and belonging and caring anchors our sense of place in the universe. Belonging is good for the brain; stress hormones are down-regulated.

Having seen quite a lot of life, I notice that two styles of thought predict catastrophe: the first is magical thinking. We have to have great respect for causality, for if you pretend that your fantasy will prevail, in all likelihood reality will take no notice and go on being reality anyhow. Hope is fine, optimism is fine, but scoffing at the evidence will cost, sometimes a lot. (See my new book *Touching a Nerve* for farm stories of such catastrophes.) The second catastrophic style of thought is pitiless, unbending, arrogant ideology. Ideology, as a set of working beliefs, can be fine, but when it is inflexible and arrogant, terrible results occur. This holds at all levels—global, national, local community, department, and the family. Judgment, reflection, and talking it over with sensible people can help orient us. It holds for political factions, religious sects, environmentalists, nutritionists, and survivalists. Balance, as Aristotle repeatedly pointed out, is an important ingredient in the good life. Wild-eyed passion about a cause can lead us into doing stupid and even tragic things. There is perhaps a place for such passion but the right places are few and far between.

For a life to be meaningful, it's enough that each day has its meaningful parts. It doesn't mean that life as a whole has to have an overarching, metaphysically-derived meaning. And the meaningfulness of one's life of course changes through time as you develop and grow, as you mature and age. As a result, life can be extraordinarily rich and so much fun. For me something that has given such joy to my life is understanding via science. Discovery has long been one of those things that I just find exquisitely exciting. I realize, of course, that not everybody shares this passion. And I realize that lots of people might think I am peculiar for finding the idea of how synapses form on spines on neurons the most thrilling thing. But given my nature, it is thrilling for me. Each person discovers their own particular kind of passion for finding something that is really beautiful and amazing and thrilling and exciting. Music maybe, acrobatics maybe, raising goats maybe. Such things also can give meaning to life.

I used to teach a course in Introductory Philosophy to undergraduates both at UC San Diego but also in Manitoba. The issue of religion very naturally would come up. In the social times after class I would go for coffee with the students. They would ask: what do you do about Christmas? And it was a very reasonable question so I explained to them thus: we really think of Christmas in terms of its original Pagan holiday, which is a celebration of winter solstice where the daylight hours are very short, but there is the expectation that the photoperiod is going to lengthen. Summer will come! Across many cultures there are various rituals associated with winter solstice, and the prospect of lengthening days is a joyful one. In our family we just partake of any ritual that happens to please us and that we feel comfortable with. Do the kids hang up stockings? Of course, and so do the dogs. Do we leave out cookies for Santa Claus? But of course. I sort of like Jesus too, because his birth is the celebration of the beauty of the newborn, and the promise that it brings for the future. I do not worry too much about the son of God aspect. The solstice customs do not have to be taken too literally; they can still be fun and playful and joyful while at the same time you know you're not buying into magic wholeheartedly. When you play Monopoly you take it all very seriously and you really want all those houses and hotels and you want to be the monopolist that wins it all, even though it's only play money. Well, in some similar way I think you can partake of various religious rituals and connect to your community without believing in the metaphysics or the mysticism or the magical stuff that goes on behind it all.

Photos: Churchland with her dogs Duff and Farley

ANTHONY B. PINN
PROFESSOR OF RELIGIOUS STUDIES, RICE UNIVERSITY
HOUSTON, TEXAS

[INTERVIEW] I'm a professor of religion, although I'm a nontheistic humanist. However, I understand that religion has played a tremendous role in the development of human thinking and doing over the course of centuries, and I think that needs to be given attention. I understand the desire on the part of many atheists or nontheistic humanists to embrace and champion science. That makes sense to me, but we also inhabit cultural worlds and we need more than natural science in order to unpack and explore those cultural worlds. So, my work within the study of religion provides a way of unpacking at least one of those cultural worlds in which we live.

I was born in the Christian church, and started preaching within the African Methodist Episcopal Church when I was about 12. I was ordained by the African Methodist Episcopal Church when I was 18 and received my second ordination shortly before going to seminary. I was involved in ministry for many of my years as a graduate student. However, I reached a point where it just no longer worked for me. It wasn't personal. It was the inability of theism to really address in a sustained way the basic needs of human communities.

It started when I was an undergraduate. I had questions concerning the nature of the gospel and how it was worked out within churches, and what that preached moment was really all about. Did the church's doctrine and theology really address the felt needs of people within the community? As an undergraduate, I was youth pastor at a rather large African Methodist Episcopal church in Brooklyn in an area called Bedford Stuyvesant, an economically challenged area at that point. And it wasn't clear to me that what we did within

the context of that church made a difference in the lived experience of people. We kind of pacified them or frightened them but we really didn't address their basic human needs in a way that spoke to the integrity of human life.

It was difficult being involved in that church but I maintained my commitment, assuming that what I was thinking about God and what God does for humans was just off and I would get it together. And that process continued as a Master of Divinity student. I was studying for the professional degree for church ministry and those questions and concerns continued. I was running into young people who were having a really difficult time; between New York and Boston I was running into young people who found it much easier to talk about their demise than their future, found it easier to write a eulogy than to outline a vast and productive life. Theism seemed to offer them no way around that situation. As a PhD student, I finally decided none of this church stuff was making sense because there really is no God. This God is a human creation along the lines of Santa Claus or the Easter Bunny, and it was able to do no more for us than Santa Claus or the Easter Bunny.

I think nontheistic humanists and atheists are much more intentional about this life, have a deeper appreciation for the ordinary elements and activities and moments of life, have a deep and abiding appreciation for the mundane, because we recognize this is all we get. And so we have to make the most of it. Something along the lines of Thoreau would argue: You have to drain from every moment as much as you can so at the end of life you know you've lived.

JOHN D. HALL
PSYCHIATRIST
CHARLOTTE, NORTH CAROLINA

One of the most important things to me and a source of joy is the search for truth. This is what eventually led to my being an atheist. When I was around 13, my mother and I attended an evangelical Methodist church. I experienced what most would consider a salvation or conversion experience on my way there one Sunday morning. I asked my mother why we went to church and she explained to me her belief in Jesus and the Christian Bible. At that time, I mentally prayed and asked to have that feeling. I experienced a warmth and peace that most in my church had described during their moment of "being saved." After that experience and up until college I prayed to God and read the Bible every night. I attended church at least weekly and even attended and eventually led a Bible Study group in my high school. I would frequently "witness" to my friends and go door-to-door with my church to tell people about Jesus and God. From these experiences, I came to understand the appeal of religious beliefs. When things were difficult (my parents' divorce, my own relationship difficulties, etc.), it was reassuring to believe in an all-powerful, benevolent God who had my back. At times it gave me peace, and it was good to have a group of people to meet with regularly and who supported one another. At times during prayer I can honestly say that I felt a connection with something greater than myself, or at least that was what I believed at the time.

During high school, I was also academically driven—making good grades in advanced courses and competing on the math and science team—and enjoyed playing soccer. Most would say I had a balanced childhood and adolescence academically, socially, and physically, and I feel fortunate to have had this opportunity since it allowed me to pursue future interests.

In college, I would often have all-night study sessions with classmates. Sometimes religion would come up, and given my Bible studies and previous experience witnessing, I thought I knew my stuff. However, instead of the blank or open looks I observed during my adolescence, I was the one getting the lessons. I received information about the history of the Old and New Testaments, learning about other religious beliefs and the contradictions in the Bible, and discussing the scientific and philosophical understanding of religion/gods. My beliefs were in complete disarray and I remember one night in particular when I was left in total confusion. At that point, I started questioning everything regarding my faith and started applying my scientific understanding to the world, including religion.

Fast forward to today. I am a psychiatrist in private practice and actively involved in public science education. I now know that the "salvation experience" I had at age 13 was based on expectation, hope, and neurobiology. I continue to experience that peace and calm that I once attributed to a god, but without the need for religious belief. I find joy and meaning in helping others overcome the pain and suffering of mental illness. In my job, I don't rely on saying "pray more" as research has shown that prayer does not work. I use proven techniques to help others achieve remission from their suffering. When I was young, religion provided a sense of community and hope during difficult times, however it was ultimately limiting. My community is now much larger and not constrained to only those who share my religious beliefs. My ethics are no longer confined to a book that contains many discriminatory, contradictory, and/or inaccurate beliefs. My morals are based on a complex understanding of myself, others, history, sociology, biology, and the other sciences, but mostly on the questions of how I can help decrease the suffering of others and myself and how I can do the most good for humanity and the world. Ultimately, religion is based on something that has no evidence for its existence and eventually anything not based in reality will collapse under better scrutiny and understanding.

I find joy in my dancing and the reason why is complex. I find joy in physical activity. Ballroom dancing is much more physically demanding than I ever thought, especially once one starts competing and performing showcases. Also, ballroom dancing requires one to engage the entire mind and body. I have to always be thinking about the current and the next step, of the other couples on the floor, of how to convey the next move to my partner, of any feedback from my partner, and of my own posture/stance—all while enjoying myself. Trust me; it's not easy, especially in the beginning, but I find joy in that challenge. In psychology, the term is optimal frustration; if a new task is too easy, nothing is learned, remembered, and/or appreciated; if a new task is too difficult, one will simply give up in frustration. I have learned that there are always deeper layers. The situation often occurs with my teacher when I feel I have finally learned a move and I really start enjoying myself. She will then tell me, "That's great, now let's learn how that move is really done!" I know she takes a perverse joy in telling me that. Eventually, I laugh with her.

Following page: Hall dancing with his partner, Laura Dunlap

YAU-MAN CHAN
CONTESTANT, *SURVIVOR: FIJI*
RETIRED DIRECTOR OF I.T. SERVICES, COLLEGE OF CHEMISTRY, UNIVERSITY OF CALIFORNIA BERKELEY
MARTINEZ, CALIFORNIA

The moon landing triggered my dedication to science. It was 1969—my last year of high school. I grew up in Borneo and we didn't even have a television. We were listening to the Voice of America radio broadcast—the live broadcast. Classes at school came to a screeching halt. Our teacher brought in a transistor radio just to listen to the lunar broadcasts. It was incredible imagining that humans were actually on the moon. We went all the way up there, and put somebody on the moon! I said, "Wow! We really can do so many of the things that we thought before were pure science fiction!" And to me, from that point on, I decided to pursue scientific knowledge and that decision has given me so many eye-opening and amazing experiences throughout the years since then. It's interesting to think of it now, that I didn't even see it on television. I was just listening to the radio—just hearing that the United States actually put these three people on a rocket and got them up there! It's really amazing. It's an experience which still stays with me to this day. That's when I decided to pursue higher education in the sciences and in the United States because they were the ones who got those men to the moon.

It's moments like that, which inspire me. The people I see around me who have dedicated their lives to the pursuit of science, to pursue knowledge which will result in better conditions for human beings. I work with research chemists who have done amazing work, some of which have benefited medical science like cancer research.

They do the fundamental research, basic research that has helped many in third world countries today with better and more effective vaccines and medications. I see graduate students and researchers who come in who are still there at three o'clock in the morning. It's their dedication. From their research, there will be hundreds and thousands of research papers written which you will never hear about. But maybe someday, someone doing some other research, maybe even totally unrelated will find those papers and their results will help them complete their understanding and advance their own finding. And to me that sort of intricate inter-relatedness of the science research discipline is quite impressive to me.

I've encountered many friends and relatives who are quite religious and superstitious, so I find myself having to occasionally answer for myself as to why I don't believe? Why don't you think it's important to do this or that ritual on Chinese New Year Eve to bring good fortune to your household and let good luck in? My reply is usually well, I've seen the world, there's so much superstition around the Chinese but guess there's people who don't even know the Chinese New Year and they live their life pretty much well and they're just as wealthy as we are, maybe even more. I'm sure Bill Gates didn't know you're not supposed to sweep the floor on New Year's Day. Fortunately, because of my environment and where I work I don't have to deal with it very often. People respect that science, reason and logic can get you very far.

JENNIFER MICHAEL HECHT
POET / HISTORIAN / PHILOSOPHER
BROOKLYN, NEW YORK

When I wrote *Doubt: A History*, I had no idea that it would have such a social aspect—through it I've heard from and spoken to a huge number of warm, fascinating people. My other new book is history and philosophy and is called *Stay: A History of Suicide and the Philosophies Against It*, which offers secular reasons that despair suicide is wrong (if you are already dying it is a different question). It too has given me a feeling of community, from the very beginning. The first iteration of these ideas came out in a poem, "The No-Hemlock Rock." I was moved by the response I got from people about that poem, and it made me want to go further with the subject.

A poet doesn't always know where a poem comes from and can be surprised by it, and one of the things I continue to find surprising in this particular poem is that when I tell the person to "rave and fail" if necessary (but don't kill yourself), I also say to "stand on a street corner/ and rhyme

seizure with Indonesia and wreck it with racket." My point is that if life gets so bad that you want to die, instead, stop trying to be normal for a while, and embrace the absurdity of it all. What catches me off guard every time I read it is that these odd rhymes make me happy. People use language every day. They stick words together and then the words fall apart again, and yet Shakespeare put, "To be or not to be" together, and those words have stayed together for four centuries. There is a kind of magic to words well joined and a powerful pleasure in attempting it.

My joy is in making art, and enjoying the art other people have made. For me, this is primarily about writing, but I also make paintings, take photographs, sculpt useless items, and create elaborate homemade jewelry for the tree in my backyard. The greatest act of creativity is, surely, just living life consciously and tending love and friendship, but I'm going to set aside that deeply

interpersonal kind of creation and talk instead about the pleasures of solitary invention.

I believe the feeling of meaning is sufficient to the definition of meaning, and the feeling of meaning comes from our community and culture and nature. It is bigger than us, and sometimes we have to have faith in it. Making art—with words or paints or things—is transcendent because you get out of the way of your controlling mind and see what comes out of your hands when you play and search for beauty and insight. It is also transcendent because it connects you with the creative action of nature and of artistic culture. It makes meaning and partakes in it.

Let me offer a poem from my new poetry book, *Who Said*.

The Spider

Spider, spider, spinning tight
against the darkness of the night,
what inspired geometry
is wonder at your web from me?

On what different leads or lies
could my sympathies arise
if, instead of these aspire,
I had but gone out there entire?

In the purpose of your art
twist the neurons of my heart.
For having lost a rhythm's beat,
I dread my hand and drag my feet.

What the knowing? What the chain?
In what furnace burns my brain?
Where's the Advil? What's to grab?
I've got your heartthrob in my bag.

When I'm the witness and the fears
fat and lean, bread, pills and tears,
and spider winding, watched by me.
And nature's this made all of we.

Spider, spider, knitting white
against the blackness of the night
what wacky-strange geometry
could frame our sweet-ass symmetry?

Most readers will recognize that this is a play on one of the most iconic poems in the English language, William Blake's "The Tyger." Blake's poem's great question to the tiger is, "Did he who made the lamb make thee?" If you believe in God, it is a central question: Whence evil? Why is the world based on so much blood and brutality, mixed somehow with majesty? My poem erupted from a real experience of watching a spider spinning an exquisite web and feeling awe and

communion with nature and creativity. She spins her web, I spin mine, we are both mortal, fleeting, and yet meaningful and real. If you don't believe in God, a central question is: Isn't it extraordinary that we experience nature as so awesome, complex, and beautiful, horrifying and sublime? Poetry is better than prose for speaking to that conundrum and all the associations it brings up because it isn't limited to expository, it can also act out a response to the question through its own

complexity and beauty and intense ideas. In *Who Said*, many poems scare me with their willingness to tell my secrets, and for some people those will be the most engaging, but I love the metaphysics of "The Spider" and the other poems like it.

For me, creative work is a combination of intense invention, research and thinking, and being connected to other people, even possibly doing some good. It makes me happy.

JOEL LEGAWIEC
PEDIATRIC NURSE
DAYTON, OHIO

When I was hit by a car in 2006, many people offered up god-related clichés. "God doesn't give you anything you can't handle." "Thank God your injuries weren't worse." Those clichés may bring comfort to believers, but I prefer knowing that I was a random victim of unfortunate circumstances rather than believing that some all-powerful deity decided I needed to suffer to fulfill part of "his plan." Thank God? No, I'm thankful for my helmet and other safety gear. They saved my life that day, even if they couldn't save my foot from amputation.

But the most challenging and most rewarding journey I've ever undertaken is the journey of parenting. Raising curious, compassionate, strong, and loving children—teaching them to love others and helping them to see the beauty of humanity—that is the most meaningful and joyful responsibility we have.

Just now we had to take a break from what we were doing, because our daughter came into the house enthusiastically telling us about how she found a bunny in the back yard and got within two feet of it. She and the bunny stared at each other for a few moments before the bunny hopped away. Our daughter was still shaking from the excitement of her encounter. Moments like this are exactly what give our life joy. Our children enjoying nature and wanting to share their experiences with us—nothing could be more perfect.

We work hard to teach them how to handle difficult times—because we all encounter adversity—what matters is how you handle it. You can be angry at a god for your misfortune, or you can recognize that life is unfair and be grateful that you get the chance to experience it at all. You can make the absolute best of life...imperfect as it is...and enjoy every second, even the tough ones.

We know this is the only life we get, so we make the most of it!

Family photo: Joel and Christi with their children Genna (left) and Cael (right)

CHRISTI LEGAWIEC
LIEUTENANT COLONEL, PILOT, UNITED STATES AIR FORCE
DAYTON, OHIO

What makes life grand is not your circumstances so much as your attitude. Joel and I know that it is the most happy of accidents that we get the privilege of living. We are grateful for the experience and tend to find enjoyment in things that others may find mundane.

We appreciate the beauty of nature and are awestruck at her power. We enjoy challenging ourselves mentally and physically. We run marathons together and take our kids and dog on hikes. I love to relax on the front porch with a good book, while Joel finds peace in problem-solving and fixing things that are broken. These are just some of the "little things" that bring us great joy. We both revel in the search for answers

to big questions. After all, just because something is unknown, doesn't mean it is unknowable.

We find meaning in trying to make the world a better place. Not to imply that we are somehow going to save the planet and everyone on it. But we hope every day that the people and places we touch are better off because we have been there. Most days, it is as simple as picking up a piece of litter, smiling at a stranger, or offering a helping hand to one in need. Joel is able to make people happier and healthier on a daily basis as a nurse.

Serving in the military is meaningful to me... defending the freedoms that enable our way of life. While there is much public debate about the

value of military service or how our government utilizes its military, I believe wholeheartedly that I am doing my part to preserve and protect the freedoms that enable each American to live a life that is uniquely theirs. To worship, or not, in whatever way they choose. Where they can speak freely, disagree with others or their own government, and argue their case for change. I have flown in combat many times; faced fear and the very real possibility of death. I did not turn to a deity to get me through those times. I relied on my training, courage, and my fellow Airmen— which I found to be far more practical than closing my eyes and hoping everything would work out all right. Yes, there are atheists in foxholes, or in this case, cockpits.

AJ JOHNSON

VICE PRESIDENT AND CO-FOUNDER, BE SECULAR
NEW YORK, NEW YORK

One of my goals in this community has always been to show people that not all atheists fit the description of atheists that is often portrayed by the media or popular culture. I am one of a growing number of atheists that are *not* heterosexual Caucasian men "of-a-certain-age." One way to see more diversity in the atheist movement is to do a better job of highlighting the diversity we have. I like to think my presence in this book (and the broader secular movement) shows people on the outside that there is a place for them. I find it inspirational to imagine, many years from now, an African American girl in the South picking this up in a library, flipping to this page, and finding an easier road to nonbelief because of my work and the work of others like me.

As a classic extrovert, I love people. Making new friends is one of my favorite things to do. During my Christian years, I was conflicted by the layered duplicity of being compelled to hate whole swaths of the population for disobeying the Word of God—and still "love everyone!" One of the greatest gifts of my nonbelief, and one of the things that makes me most happy, is truly feeling like I am able to be more accepting of people. An action is no longer reprehensible because it is a "sin," it is reprehensible because it wrongly hurt someone else. The ability to apply rationality to behavior is not a priority in the religious world, but it's one of the underlying principles of secular humanism.

The one thing I'd like to help people understand is that atheists are not very different from anyone else (even in some of the ways we might like to be). Although it's fantastic, being an atheist isn't the only thing that makes us happy. I enjoy most of the same things most people enjoy, and I'm sure the same is true for you. I love listening to live music, playing instruments (esp. bass guitar), eating good food, falling in love, singing loudly with the windows down, making people laugh, and doing the right thing—because my mother taught me to, not because "God is watching." On the negative side, being an atheist doesn't make all of us less susceptible to the same tribalism, sexism, stereotyping, or any other mental biases and heuristics. Atheists fall prey to homeopathic scams, as well as UFO and other half-baked conspiracies. Not all atheists are skeptics or humanists, and not all "skeptics" and "humanists" are good at it.

My Internet nickname is "Happiest Atheist," and I think the label is confusing for some. This is because I do not consider myself to be the #1 *happiest* atheist in the entire universe (although I would probably rank near the top). Rather, I've found my life to be an overall better and more enjoyable experience since I've become an atheist. I am my happiest as an atheist. After giving dozens of speeches and attending numerous conferences within the Freethought Movement, I do not think this position is unique. I think a lot of people are happier after losing their religion—and that makes me even happier.

DONALD C. JOHANSON
PALEOANTHROPOLOGIST, ARIZONA STATE UNIVERSITY / DISCOVERER OF "LUCY"
TEMPE, ARIZONA

[INTERVIEW] Having the opportunity to be alive gives me joy every day. With only minor changes in your DNA you would be somebody else and never be you. To have the privilege of having this one life is remarkable. Many things give me pleasure in this life. Watching a sunset on the Serengeti, or landing in Addis Ababa, Ethiopia at sunrise, flying over the Sudan and seeing the light reflect off of the Nile. There's beauty everywhere and it's just such a turn-on to be alive.

We live on the "Pale Blue Dot" in the infinite universe and I remember was when I was in high school and we had a telescope, a really big, good telescope. Built in the late 1800s. And I think that was the first time I looked through a telescope of that size and saw the four moons of Jupiter and realized that one of the great heretics, Galileo, was the guy who realized these were moons. And what was even more exciting about it was I turned to someone who was with me, who said, "I don't see four moons, there's only three." And I looked back and sure enough there were only three. We mulled this over and of course one of them had just gone behind Jupiter. I thought, how remarkable! I wanted to share that knowledge about the solar system we live in, and I saved my newspaper money to buy a little four-inch reflecting telescope that I would set up on the street where I lived in Connecticut. People would come along and they all had that 'aha' moment. They'd look through it and say, "Oh, wow!" I said, "Yeah, those are the moons of Jupiter, the Galilean moons." The wonder of natural world around us has captivated me my whole life. Mapping the moon's craters, looking at the transit of Venus, these are moments that bring an enormous amount of joy to me.

The seminal moment in my life, that led to a lifelong career as an anthropologist, happened when I was a young teenager. I knew instantly when I read Thomas Henry Huxley's book *Man's Place in Nature* that I wanted to find fossilized remains of our earliest ancestors. These moments are rare, but defining. The basic premise in the book—that we are all part of the natural world and that we and the African apes shared a

common ancestor in the distant past—blew my mind. Evolution became the paradigm in which I have viewed the natural world ever since. This is such a robust theory that it explains the entire biological world on this planet—pretty elegant stuff.

Huxley and Charles Darwin made the prediction that the most ancient and ape-like human ancestors would be found in Africa where the apes live today. This prediction was proven correct in 1924 when the fossil skull of an early human, the Taung Baby, was found in South Africa.

In hindsight, Huxley and Darwin's prognostication was based on anatomical observations of chimp and human bodies. They knew nothing about DNA and only had the original fossil Neanderthal from Germany to consider as a fossil human. It is a testament to their prowess and the strength of the evolutionary paradigm that they made the prediction and it was tested and found out to be true.

My childhood dream to find ancient human fossils was immeasurably rewarded in 1974 when I found Lucy, a 3.2 million-year-old partial skeleton in Ethiopia. That moment defined who I was.

All this looks so straightforward on the pages of National Geographic, but the trials and tribulations I had to navigate through were often daunting. One of my mottos in life is that "the road to success is always under construction." One has to bring passion, persistence, and a deep belief in yourself to attain success. I got a lot of this from my late mother who demonstrated a remarkable level of strength as she raised me after the untimely death of my father when I was only two years old.

My lifelong dedication to paleoanthropology came largely from Paul Leser, an professor of anthropology I met when I was nine. Born in Germany he fled to Sweden during Nazism. These two people, my mother and Leser, taught me to follow my dreams, develop a passion, take charge and be proactive. The support and guidance they

gave me at every critical moment in my life gave me the confidence I needed to move forward.

My science has been perhaps the most important thing in my life. Not just because of finding something like Lucy, but because these finds not only tie us to the past, but they tie us to the natural world around us. As an undergraduate taking my first anthropology course at the University of Illinois, we used a book by an anthropologist named Alfred Kroeber. He thought that humans were "super-organic"—implying that we were outside of nature largely because we based our survival on our capacity for culture. I recall arguing with my professor for Huxley's view of our place in nature. What I do as a paleoanthropologist gives me such incredible joy because I know we are documenting our place in nature.

There's no argument that we are the most intelligent and the most powerful creature on the planet. But in many respects we have turned our back on the natural world. We must reinvent a reverence for the natural world before we damage it so much that our existence will be in peril. The natural world is going to run out before we run out. Sooner rather than later there will be no clean air, no drinkable water, a shortage of food to eat and not enough space to live.

Humans think they are invulnerable and free from extinction, but just as a cataclysmic event killed off the dinosaurs, it could happen to us. When you immerse yourself in the natural world, in the universe, you realize we really are part of it, and we can't escape it. We must appreciate the natural world, protect it and understand we are part of the whole process of life on this planet. It is vitally important for us as a species to understand we are part of the fabric of the natural world. Our species, that I sometimes call *Homo egocentricus*, must responsibly embrace our responsibilities to our planet and stop acting as if there was another place in the universe for us to move to after we have trashed mother earth.

Following page: Johanson with a replica of the skull of his most famous discovery, the Australopithecus afarensis known as "Lucy"

MARGARET DOWNEY
SECULAR OFFICIANT / FOUNDER AND PRESIDENT, THE FREETHOUGHT SOCIETY
POCOPSON, PENNSYLVANIA

My passion to learn has never stopped. I hope to be the type of person who will be doing an Internet search for more knowledge until the day I die. I imagine myself in my 90s wrapped in a cozy blanket, using the latest technological gadget to examine and comprehend the newest scientific discovery and feeling great joy in knowing more facts. I have never been the type of person who is satisfied with a far-fetched story to explain the unexplainable.

Questioning and investigation brings me great satisfaction. While I am not a scientist, learning about any given subject provides me with insight, appreciation and knowledge that make life enjoyable and interesting. This is a wonderful time to be alive. Unlimited answers are just an Internet search away.

Learning, thinking and activism keep me young. Knowledge about the natural world made me very aware that my life is finite and there may soon be physical restraints in the way I live. This is why I often volunteer my time for community improvement efforts such as road cleanup efforts, stacking food at a women's shelter, packing food cartoons for the needy, collecting clothes for the homeless and fundraising for victims of disasters. I am following my passion to be a part of a problem-solving community that includes civil rights concerns and upholding America's constitutional principles of freedom and justice. Being an involved, informed and concerned citizen brings me joy. I love my country more than any god.

Ah, love—the emotional state that makes life wonderful. I have great affection for people, animals, concepts and things. This is probably why I find great joy in the creation of secular ceremonies. The nontheist community is comprised of many people who enjoy acknowledging life passages such as marriage, birth, coming of age, holiday observances, anniversaries, and funerals. I help create personal, religion-free texts for those special occasions. I can't describe the joy and meaning I find in helping fellow nontheists celebrate important events in their lives. My entire body is bathed up in happiness as I gaze upon a couple getting married or when I witness the sweetness of a baby's face as "Guide Parents" are named and his or her birth or adoption is acknowledged.

Secular holidays are also important to many nontheists and I am proud to have created a winter holiday symbol that has been adopted across the world. In 2007, the Freethought Society placed a large evergreen tree in a West Chester, Pennsylvania free speech zone. The ornaments on the tree are laminated color copies of book covers. They sparkle in the sunlight during the day and they glimmer in the glow of a nighttime spotlight. The wide varieties of books on display illustrate what all nontheists advocate: "With knowledge all things can be understood."

Our display conveys to others that we are an integral part of society and not a silent minority. We strive to be accepted, included and understood. Books about history, science, philosophy, life narratives, technology, and ancient mythology promote the educational value we hold dear. I want to see, in my lifetime, additional international versions of The Tree of Knowledge being used as a nontheist winter holiday symbol.

I am optimistic that, with more knowledge of the natural world, humans will evolve into a more tolerant and peaceful society. It is my hope that my actions throughout my life will contribute to social advances and that I will serve as a role model by working hard, being dedicated to a cause and joyfully exemplifying nontheist principles.

LAWRENCE M. KRAUSS

FOUNDATION PROFESSOR AND DIRECTOR, ORIGINS PROJECT AT ARIZONA STATE UNIVERSITY
TEMPE, ARIZONA

[INTERVIEW] I get joy in discovering aspects of the universe and how remarkable the universe is. I get joy in learning every day that the universe is more amazing and surprising than I ever imagined. And I get meaning from the fact that there is no meaning, the fact that there's no purpose to the universe. The meaning in my life is the meaning I make. I'm lucky enough to be here, as we all are, and I have a consciousness and some brief amount of time to make the most of it. And so meaning in my life is literally that. It's the fact that I try and make the most out of my life from a personal perspective of experiencing the world in every way that I can, and also to have an impact on the world that's positive for not just my children but for other people who live here.

To me, that meaning is so much more real than presuming someone else defines meaning to my life. I think that's one of the reasons why I'm an anti-theist. I wouldn't want to live in a universe with a supreme being who pulled all the strings and was like a cosmic Saddam Hussein, condemning people not just for their life but for all eternity if they make mistakes. Many religions talk about flocks and sheep, but who would want to be a sheep? I think the fact that we're here to make meaning, and that what we do is up to us, should invigorate us. It invigorates me. I feel invigorated every day by the fact that I can make my own impacts and I can get my own joy.

I would argue that the spiritual fulfillment many religious people claim they get is really something they're imagining in order to be able to achieve the same thing you could get without it. And when most people say that they're religious, it has a different meaning for every person. As my friend Stephen Weinberg has said, people want to believe in believing. Most people who adhere to a certain religion don't buy the doctrines of that religion. They don't believe when a priest blesses a wafer it turns into the body of a first century Jew. They don't believe that stuff. They don't believe Jonah was swallowed by a whale. They don't believe the sun sat still in the sky when a horn blew. They say, well, I like this and I don't like that, so I'll throw out the things I don't like and I'll call it my religion. Well that's just people saying I find solace in what I read. And I find solace in the universe.

It makes me incredibly happy, the idea that there's no afterlife. I can't think of a worse curse than to be eternally surrounded by my friends and family and people I don't like as well. I think it's invigorating that we have this time on earth to do what we can do. The idea of putting off all happiness to some later time is not good from my point of view. It may allow you to accept an unfair universe in which you're treated poorly and be more stoic about it. And I think that was the great effect of religion. It took people who were poor and had no future and allowed them to somehow get resigned to that life. But I think that recognizing that you weren't here before you were born, and that your consciousness won't be here after you die, implies that every moment is more precious. And what you do here on earth matters more because you won't have any opportunity afterwards to fix it up.

There is poetry in nature. The universe is far more poetic than the Bible or any of the scriptures in so many ways, because the real story is so much more fascinating than the rather mundane story invented by human beings. This is because the imagination of the universe is far greater than our human imagination and it always surprises us, which is why we keep having to go out and ask questions. The difference between science and religion is that we don't presume the answers before we ask the questions. We keep learning from the universe. And if we just locked ourselves in a room scribbling down theoretical physics as opposed to scriptures we'd still come up with the wrong answer. We need to constantly get the check of reality.

And one of the more poetic things about the universe (I wrote a whole book about it) is that we're stardust. We all come from the stars. That every atom in our bodies experienced the most violent cosmic fireworks in the universe, and the atoms in your left hand may have come from a different star than your right hand because all the heavy elements beyond lithium, carbon, nitrogen, oxygen, and all the things that matter were only created in stars. So to get in our body, they had to have been created in a star, which then exploded and died so we would be here. And I made a joke saying, forget Jesus, the *stars* died so you'd be born. And it's caught on, but independent of that facetiousness, the point is that we are directly connected to the cosmos in an intimate way, and all of our atoms have experienced the most amazing violent and remarkable explosions in nature, billions of years ago, and will be around for billions of years to come—and that's our connection to the universe that verges on being eternal. It's not eternal, but that's our long-lived connection to the universe. For me, *that* poetry is far more remarkable than some silly story by an Iron Age peasant.

Photo: Krauss in his office, holding a globe of the cosmic microwave background radiation

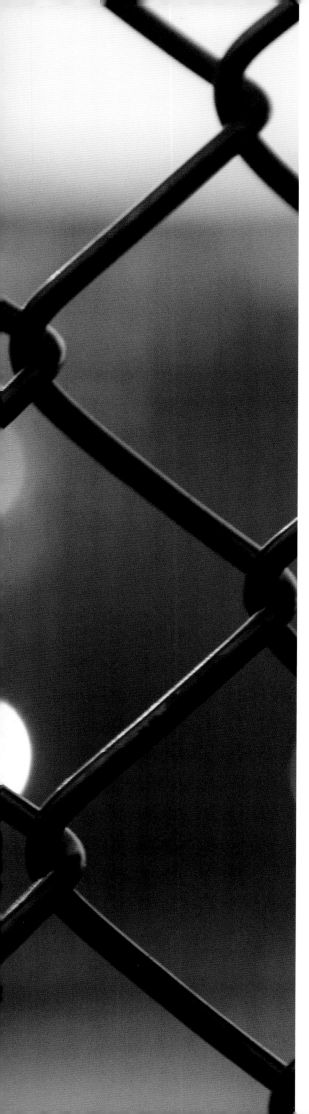

DIANNE ARELLANO
PHOTO DOCUMENTARIAN / YOUTH ADVOCACY EDUCATOR
LOS ANGELES, CALIFORNIA

SIKIVU HUTCHINSON
AUTHOR / EDUCATOR
LOS ANGELES, CALIFORNIA

We are openly identified atheists working in black and brown communities, where the lives of children of color are devalued and far too many are pipelined into prisons. As feminists of color, our joy and purpose come from activism, namely teaching, serving and shaping the next generation of humanist intellectuals and leaders from schools that have been written off as expendable, "ghetto," dangerous and low-achieving. Far too often, humanism is not culturally relevant for people of color. It's perceived as white and disconnected from the real circumstances of youth who are automatically criminalized by mainstream society's racist misperceptions. Despite the rhetoric of colorblind post-racialism, the wealth gap between whites and African Americans and Latinos has grown to epic proportions, and upward mobility for people of color is more elusive.

Despite the rhetoric of post-feminism, the rates of sexual assault, HIV/AIDS contraction and intimate partner violence amongst young women of color are exploding. These are moral obscenities which most humanism-espousing atheists have failed to address and have the luxury to remain ignorant of. Clearly, a so-called secular democracy that is also the wealthiest, most prolific jailer of black people in the world cannot claim to be a beacon of liberty and justice for all. As educators and mentors for the Women's Leadership Project, a feminist humanist advocacy program, we've been privileged to work with brilliant students who are pushing back against the dominant culture's stereotypes about women of color as hyper-sexual welfare queens, "sluts" and maids.

We've had college counselors tell our students not to even think about applying to college because they are undocumented or in foster care. We've had teachers automatically steer girls of color who showed high aptitude in science into nursing. We've seen young women and men who have been written off academically come into their own as speakers, leaders and trainers on sexual assault, reproductive justice, black/brown solidarity, homophobia and HIV/AIDS education. One of our greatest sources of joy has been seeing our mentees then turn around and teach their peers to make connections between their lived experiences and the broader conditions of racism, sexism, classism, heterosexism and religious bigotry.

This is the kind of critical thinking, engaged politics and social obligation that culturally relevant humanism emphasizes. And contrary to the religionists who claim God's will shapes purpose, every day that we can wake up and learn from these young, unsung visionaries is a deeply purposeful one.

Photo: Arellano (left) and Hutchinson (right)

KEVIN DAVIS
CHURCH-STATE BLOGGER
CHURCHVILLE, NEW YORK

There was a time in my life when my search for answers resulted in becoming a "saved" Christian. During this period, I was taught that joy and meaning in my life should come from the Bible, my Christian leaders and peers, and my personal relationship with Jesus. That was the same time in my life that my thirst for knowledge started to take shape. I wanted to know more about my Christian faith, and I was in search of more truth. My journey brought me through college courses on theology and philosophy, as well as the sciences of anthropology and geology. I found more proof and wisdom in science and reason than in the mythical, supernatural tall tales of the Bible. I didn't choose to be an atheist. I simply became more educated about origins—the origin of man, the origin of the earth, and more eye-opening than anything, the origin of the Bible, the gospels, Christianity, and other religions.

I began to think freely and base my beliefs on truth, facts, and reason. I started to see the hypocrisy of religion and those involved with it. I learned more about the damage caused by religion: the wars, the endless violence, oppression, and inhibition of progress. My eyes were finally open and I was free.

Over the years since, I've grown more comfortable with being known as an atheist among my family and friends, despite the overwhelming societal taboo of the term. I've found joy and meaning in running a blog focused on keeping the influence of religious doctrine out of our government and public schools. Through my blog, *Divided Under God*, it's my mission to bring awareness to current church/state separation issues and discuss how these issues affect all of us and our children. I've found meaning in knowing that I'm doing something positive to make the world around me a better place for my son and any future children. I've found joy in the positive feedback I get from readers, who in turn pass the information and perspective on to others so that we can all be vigilant and mindful of those who insist on bringing religious doctrine into government and schools, replacing science, reason, and progress.

All atheists come to the realization that an "afterlife" is something that is fictional and used by religions to motivate their followers, but also to frighten and control them at times. For many, the lack of an afterlife is a difficult concept to accept, especially considering some atheists' level of prior indoctrination. Being atheists forces us to accept our own mortality. However, accepting my own mortality has helped me to find joy and meaning in the life I am living. I live in the present, rather than living for the promise of better things to come. I focus on enjoying the time I have with my family and friends, especially my wife and son. I treat people with kindness, compassion, and respect because it's the right and humane thing to do, not because it will earn me eternal reward. I will teach my son *how* to think, not *what* to think, and he will be better for it. I won't waste my time on earth in a selfish quest to gain the approval of a god that no one can prove the existence of. Instead, I will spend my short time in this world doing what I can to make it better for the people I love and earn my place in their hearts and memories.

ROY SPECKHARDT

EXECUTIVE DIRECTOR, AMERICAN HUMANIST ASSOCIATION
WASHINGTON, D.C.

As someone who is contemplative and comfortable working independently, I have great appreciation for things I can do on my own. I love to experience beautiful natural scenes, from meadows to mountaintops, from beaches to bubbling brooks. I feel accomplishment when I complete a budgeting process or do my taxes and the numbers match up—whether or not I have to pay! I enjoy the feeling of righteousness I share in when I hear presentations by people like Harvey Milk, Quentin Tarantino, Toni Morrison, or Gloria Steinem. And I share in the feeling of success when I see Reggie Bush pinwheel and stiff-arm his way to a touchdown. But, I find that my greatest inspiration comes from my relationships with others.

Sometimes those relationships are fleeting but substantive, like the time I shared a lunch with Salman Rushdie, who I saw sitting by himself in the lunch room at the New Humanism Conference at Harvard. Getting the chance to see his lightning-fast and unfathomably deep thought process gave me a new perspective on the heights we can reach in our intellectual development. On a similar occasion, I shared a dinner with Julia Sweeney, who was so delightful and funny and genuinely interested in hearing my story about my personal path to humanism that I was all the more blown away by her hilarious exploration of her letting go of God.

Of course, who could be closer than the person you've agreed to spend the rest of your life with? I wouldn't be able to face network television cameras, share my innermost opinions on the world around me in columns, or lead with deliberation without the confidence and support that I get from Maggie Ardiente. There is no joy like the joy I get from spending ordinary time with her, and there's no meaning and purpose like the unwavering drive I have to do what I can to share happiness with her. Everything I look forward to experiencing is made better by her presence.

In between the fleeting and the unending are relationships that build over the years. For me, local humanist leaders and donors that I see annually are like friendly relatives who become increasingly part of my life and work. Among them are instinctive leaders from whom I try to learn, fast friends who display their loyalty and support, and even therapists who may know me better than me.

So, for me, I get inspiration from many sources, but personal relationships with friends and loved ones are what really raise me up to a level that I could not achieve without them. And so that's what matters most to me, and gives me the energy to do what I do.

MAGGIE ARDIENTE
DIRECTOR OF DEVELOPMENT AND COMMUNICATIONS, AMERICAN HUMANIST ASSOCIATION
WASHINGTON, D.C.

I love everything about food. It encompasses so many wonderful ideals: the adventure of trying something new, experimenting with your taste buds to determine what you like and don't like, enjoying a hearty meal on a winter night, enjoying drinks outside during the warm summer months, the pride that comes with finishing a perfectly home-cooked dish, and the ability to gather friends and family together over a meal—without the need to say grace, of course.

My husband and colleague at the American Humanist Association, Roy Speckhardt, and I dine out a lot as part of our work. Sitting across the table from a fellow atheist over a meal and talking about our mutual passion for humanism is my favorite part of the job. I've gotten to know hundreds of humanists on a personal level over the years, and I'm grateful to them for opening up their homes, for taking the time to learn more about our organization, and for their generous donations that make our work possible.

At my alma mater, James Madison University, I was vice president of the JMU Freethinkers, a student club for atheists, agnostics, and humanists. Being a nonbeliever was a big part of my identity on campus. We celebrated Darwin Day with lectures on evolution, protested when conservative religious figures like Roy Moore visited campus, and raised money for secular charities like Doctors Without Borders. We even had a "Freethinker House" where several club members and I lived our senior year. We had a blast.

After I graduated, I knew I wanted to work for a cause: civil liberties, women's rights, marriage equality, or countless other issues that were very important to me. When I learned about humanism—the idea that you can be good without a belief in a god—I discovered that I didn't have to work for just one particular cause. The American Humanist Association already encompassed all the progressive issues I already cared so much about, and I realized religion often played a role in the curtailing of human rights. I get to be an atheist *and* make the world a better place! So to be able to translate my passion for humanism into a full-time career is just icing on what already is a very delicious cake. (See, I always find ways to incorporate food into everything!)

Whenever I think of the many things in life that give me joy, it always involves being with someone and sharing new experiences together. It's only inevitable that my career would be about just that: meeting new people and sharing in the joy of being humanists together. It pleases me to no end that Roy in particular shares in my joy of life's many pleasures. And I count myself very lucky to contribute to the atheist movement in a meaningful way.

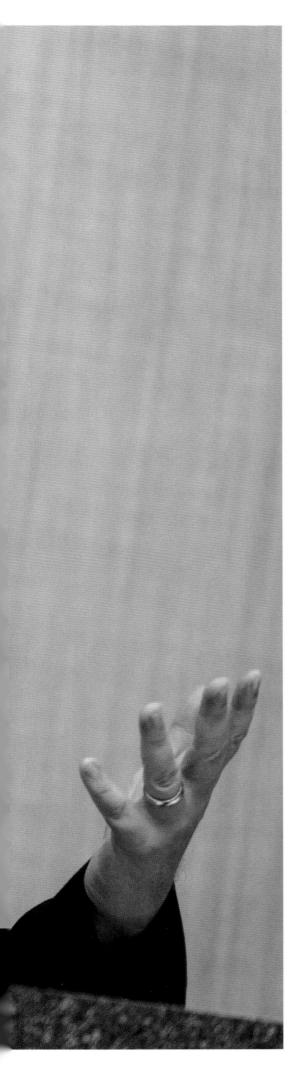

PZ MYERS
BIOLOGIST
MORRIS, MINNESOTA

[INTERVIEW] I've been married for 32 years now. I've got three kids. If you asked me what the most important thing in the world is, it's the relationship with those people in my life. Science also gives a lot of meaning to my life because what I dedicated my life to is figuring out what the real answers are. How does the world really work, particularly biology? That's my interest. Where did we come from? How are we here like this? What makes us tick? That's really cool and exciting. That's what I get into. Then, of course, I would say I find satisfaction from community with people around me. One of the goals of atheists has to be improving the quality of our social networks. That's what builds this whole framework together and stitches us into one piece so we can accomplish great things. For so many years atheists have been sort of the curmudgeonly type, the solitary loners. That doesn't work if you want to bring about social change.

There are many people who will say all atheism means is that you don't believe in God. And that's not true. I know it's not true for them because you just don't suddenly get this idea out of nowhere that, oh, there's no God. There are things, there are forces, and there are ideas that drove you to that position. And so I think it's far more interesting to explain how you came to that position. Why are you thinking that way? Like I said, "atheist" is inadequate. It's a short, quick term but it's only preliminary. There's much more that has to be said to explain what you are, because when you say you're an atheist, what you have done is thrown away the holy father in the sky who's passing down laws. You're saying that doesn't happen. You're also throwing away the afterlife. You're saying that there are no consequences after you're dead. What you have to do then is to find new reasons to behave as you do. You can no longer do it by dogma and authority.

In evolutionary biology, we understand that contingency and chance are important in putting us here. And on the religious side, you so often hear that it's destiny, fate, that God has a plan for you. That's why you're here. That's the antithesis of what we think. If you read Rick Warren's *Purpose Driven Life*, that stuff is scary, that's horrible. My nightmare is a life where I have one purpose, which is to serve this supreme tyrant in the sky, and my reward for getting through this life and navigating this life is to spend an eternity in servility. No, I'd much prefer the chance driven life, the occasional accident, that there's actually no purpose at all for being here except what purpose I can find for myself.

I spend my life making the atheist family stronger and happier. That's a good thing. But I also think it's more than just happiness. It's service, having a cause. I sit back and meditate and when I'm just trying to put myself into another place and relax for a little while, one of the things I like to think about is what would be life be like 100 years from now? I realize I'm not here, I'm long dead by then, that's far enough in the future that even my kids will be dead, which is kind of horrifying. But I can find some satisfaction and joy in thinking hoping people are still here. I hope we still have communities getting together and dancing or listening to music or talking about books. These are the kinds of things I find a lot of satisfaction in. It's not like transcendent joy; it's just good to think of the world as we know it going on in some form or another.

ARON RA
TEXAS STATE DIRECTOR, AMERICAN ATHEISTS
AUTHOR, *FOUNDATIONAL FALSEHOODS OF CREATIONISM*
GARLAND, TEXAS

Anytime I hear someone say that only humans have a thoughtful mind, a loving heart, or a compassionate soul, I have to think that person has never owned a dog or known an elephant. They preach against evolution saying, "If you tell people they're animals, they'll act like animals." Good, they should. Only humans are capable of 'inhuman' cruelty.

One of the difficulties I have in relating to other people is that I really don't understand negative perspectives like loneliness or depression. I feel good all the time, and my mood is normally pretty good, too. But I have usually been very poor and I know what hardships others are going through that are worse than anything I ever endured. I understand the big picture well enough that it has given me a sense of perspective. Someone I knew long ago held the philosophy that, "those who refuse to accept anything but the very best very often get it." I don't think so. I think such people are likely to die disappointed. No matter how good things are, they could always be better. Thinking that way means never being able to enjoy your life as it is. Then there are those who say, "You don't know what you've got 'til it's gone." I think that's stupid too. I think those

people are living in the past, and they weren't living that well when it was their present. I'm aware of every advantage I have, and I make the most of what I've got while I've got it.

That's why my wife and I still celebrate Thanksgiving; we want ourselves and our kids to appreciate every aspect of life. That way of thinking will improve your attitude! If you can't find a positive side to something you're dealing with, at least allow yourself to be impressed. If you're going to live life, love it, and try not to complain. Seriously, no one cares what you hate and you shouldn't either. It is only the things you love that will endear you in the memory of others, so that when someone is reminded of those things, they're reminded of you. That's the closest thing to immortality we'll ever have, whatever difference we made in the lives of those around us.

And I'm happy with that.

Main photo: Ra with his dogs Sugar and Moka
Family photo: (left to right) Ra's children Xavier, Meghan and Logan, wife Lilandra & son Connor

204

CHRIS STEDMAN

ASSISTANT HUMANIST CHAPLAIN, HARVARD UNIVERSITY / COORDINATOR OF HUMANIST LIFE, YALE UNIVERSITY
SOMERVILLE, MASSACHUSETTS

[INTERVIEW] One of the places in which I most immediately experience awe and wonder is out in nature. I grew up in Minnesota—the "land of 10,000 lakes"—so that feels like home to me. I feel small, finding significance in my insignificance. But I also feel a similar sense of wonder when I look at human achievement and consider what humans have created. Of course, human achievement has contributed to the destruction of our planet and we must be mindful of and do something about that, but I am continually amazed by the fact that human minds have come up with, for example, the technology that enables me to stay in touch with my mother, who lives thousands and thousands of miles away.

When I stop to reflect and consider the world around me, and the people that inhabit it—on my relationships with other people, what I have learned and experienced due to the abilities of others—I feel a sense of awe. When I am able to transcend my selfish instincts and do something to help others—to collaborate and work with others toward advancing the common good, to learn from the experiences of others—I feel it. When I think of the selfless acts that others have done for me, like all of the support that my mother and so many others have shown for me over the years, I am overcome with gratitude. Humans are relational creatures. We can compose meaning in community—by being in a relationship with one another. If there are no gods or supernatural creatures, we are all we have. Thus, we must treat one another with kindness and compassion.

One of the most visceral memories I have of feeling a sense of wonder about my atheism is how I felt when I read a number of Carl Sagan's writings for the first time. His work really resonates with me. I have a tattoo of one of his quotes on my right arm, "For small creatures such as we the vastness is bearable only through love." (That same quote also opens my book, *Faithiest: How an Atheist Found Common Ground with the Religious*.) Sagan was able to take these emotional experiences of awe and wonder and put them into words in a way that connects with my understanding of these sensations much more than anything I ever read as a Christian. His work is one example of the way in which learning new things gives me that sense of wonder.

Because as human beings we must rely on one another, I would love to see a community of atheists, agnostics, and nonreligious people who are able to have very honest and forthright conversations about our disagreements, but then sit down and break bread together—where we can be in community with one another and learn from those disagreements. I have found in my work in the interfaith movement that it can be extremely valuable to talk openly about important disagreements while also recognizing that there are things that we agree about, as well.

It might seem superficial or obvious to acknowledge that there are things that we agree about before getting to the things we disagree about, but it can make a significant difference. It can be hugely symbolic for people to say, "I don't agree with you but I respect and admire you as a person. I think that you have valuable insights to offer. I think there are things that we agree on, and because of these things I trust that we can aspire to talk about the things that we disagree on in a way that is civil and compassionate." This kind of environment, where people are actually striving to learn from one another, creates a space for learning. I would like to see a greater emphasis in the atheist movement on rational and compassionate discussions about disagreements, and a more diverse set of experiences and ideas lifted up as an important part of the movement.

My job title is Humanist Chaplain, but what I really am is a community organizer. What I try to do in the atheist, agnostic, and secular community is talk with members of our community about what they are interested in and what they value. What kind of conversations do they want to be having as a community? What kind of activism do they want to be doing? After I collect this information, I work with them and try to help make those things happen. We all have very busy lives. We're frequently plugged in, distracted, half-present. There are often more things vying for our attention than we can even begin to respond to. So I think having people whose job it is to help take these ideas and translate them into something tangible can help support a community's growth—having people who are responsible for taking the temperature of the community, finding out what people are interested in, and helping to make those things a reality.

It's a great thrill to get to do that work, because the people in our nontheist community have such great ideas and are passionate about so many things. It's a real privilege to get to help make those things happen. Having people who can help support the nontheist community in that way—having the kinds of resources that religious communities often have—will help the growth of grassroots, local, secular communities. In turn, these nonreligious communities will be well-positioned to be in conversation with religious communities—to break down barriers and build coalitions, to destigmatize the nonreligious by building relationships and sharing stories, to identify areas of shared concern and work together across lines of difference to improve the world. As an atheist, I see no evidence to suggest that a divine or supernatural force will intervene in human affairs and solve our problems for us. Thus, we have to work with others—religious and nonreligious alike—toward realizing a more just world.

Feeling awe is wonderful, but it can be that much more wonderful when we experience and share it with others in community.

MARTIN WAGNER
FILM PRODUCER AND DIRECTOR
CO-HOST, *THE ATHEIST EXPERIENCE*
AUSTIN, TEXAS

Of all human virtues, I consider honesty the most important. Honesty forces me to confess that I have lapsed into dishonesty many times in my life. We are flawed beings, we humans. You might tell a little white lie to a parent or loved one from the most benign motives because they may worry about you if they knew the truth. You may say a job interview went great, when you didn't get it at all. You make excuses for life's little dishonesties but inside they still nag at you. Or they should.

But there is a greater dishonesty, and that is lying to yourself. Many people live with lies at the core of their being. Some don't know this and deserve sympathy and kindness. Some do know but do it anyway, and I have some sympathy for them as well, because it must be a confused and unhappy charade they are forcing themselves to play out, day by day.

I am an atheist, but I got that way by embracing reason and skepticism first. Those are honesty's front line troops in the battle for your mind. I decided, at a crucial period in my life, that it really mattered whether the things I believed were actually true and not just existentially comforting.

I question relentlessly. I pursue knowledge. I know I have biases, and I do my best to recognize them and not let them grip me too tightly. I see people clinging to biases they cherish, even when they've had it demonstrated to them those biases have no truth to them, and they struggle. They fear unhappiness, a loss of direction and purpose if the dogmas they've been taught as children are stripped from them. They've been sold a false idea of happiness, one that reminds me of George Bernard Shaw's great quote: "The fact that a believer is happier than a skeptic is no more to the point than the fact that a drunken man is happier than a sober one."

Being dishonest to yourself is like always wanting to be drunk. You cannot derive happiness from sober reality, so you must shield yourself in a world of delusion and altered reality. I hope it makes you happy. If I have to trade off that approach to happiness for the relationship to reality that honesty demands of me—one that is often messy, not always affirming of my biases, or of my personal need for validation and self-importance, one that forces me to confront both the pleasant and the unpleasant in the world— then, as imperfect as it may be, I think I have a better life.

SOHAILA SHARIFI
WOMEN'S RIGHTS ACTIVIST, EQUAL RIGHTS NOW
LONDON, UNITED KINGDOM

One of the first memories in my life is of my father's deep melodic voice, reciting the Quran early each morning. He taught me how to pray and read the Quran when I turned six. Every morning, he taught me a small verse and asked me to recite the previous day's verse. He then would briefly give me a lesson on the pillars and teachings of Islam, and make me review the most important prayers. By the age of nine, I had read a great deal of the Quran, learnt a long list of rules and was familiar with the history of Islam. My father was proud of my progress and would often express his regret that I was not a boy since, according to him, I would have made a good Islamic scholar. It was obvious that Allah was not very keen on girls. There was a long list of things they were not allowed to do and apparently there was something so shameful about their bodies and hair that God ordered them to cover up, especially when appearing in front of him for prayers. It bothered me a great deal that my little brother was allowed to stand in the front alongside my father to pray, while mum and I had to stand a few feet behind them. When I asked the adults about this, I was told that the rules were made by God and there was no questioning His wisdom.

It was the great upheaval of the 1979 Iranian revolution that made it possible for me and many others to raise our long-suppressed questions about religion, God and the order of the world, and to search for answers. No matter how the Islamic regime tried to suppress freedom and everything that our revolution stood for, no matter how hard they tried to establish the absolute rule of God, no matter how horrific their prisons were and how many people they killed, they could not take away what we had gained in those few years of revolution; we had shed ourselves of the firm grip of God and as a result had been set free— free to look for alternatives, free to say no and free to dream and fight for a better life.

This, for me, has been a source of great joy. I feel proud and happy to be part of a global movement for secularism and humanity. I feel joy when I realise that I am following in the footsteps of many great people who have fought for freedom throughout history.

MICHAEL DE DORA

DIRECTOR OF DOMESTIC AND INTERNATIONAL POLICY, CENTER FOR INQUIRY
WASHINGTON, D.C.

Like most people in the world, I was raised to believe in a God. I was born into in a Roman Catholic family, so the God I grew up to believe in was all-powerful, all-knowing, and all-good. He took care of those faithful to him and his values, both protecting them on Earth and providing them eternal bliss after death.

I firmly believed in this God until I went college, at which point I was confronted with a surprisingly wide range of views on religion. Intrigued by this, I began to read more about the world's religions. Soon enough, I had doubts regarding the merits of my own faith. By the time I graduated from college and entered the workforce, I had discarded my religious beliefs as unsupportable and accepted that I was an atheist.

On the surface, my life is not very different from when I was religious. For instance, despite some initial difficulties, I have remained in a loving relationship with my family. I have remained close with many of the same great friends I've been lucky enough to have since childhood. And I still enjoy hobbies such as baseball, music, reading, writing, and exploring nature.

However, soon after becoming an atheist I did notice a significant change in my perspective and motivations. I used to believe that God would take care of everything; that this life was simply a pre-cursor to eternity. I no longer believed those things. My new perspective was that humans are responsible for taking care of each other; that this life is all that matters.

This new perspective sparked within me a new and intense dedication to living my best life now, and helping others to do the same. I believe it also increased my satisfaction in existing pursuits and experiences, and pushed me into new areas of interest.

Putting religious explanations aside, I began to develop a deep curiosity in science and philosophy. I now actively seek out scientific evidence and theories on how life on earth began and evolved, how and why life operates as it does, and even how this universe came to exist in this fashion in the first place. In turn, I have developed a new appreciation for nature. Recently, I was at the Grand Canyon—how incredible to stand before a miles-wide and miles-deep valley and think that it was formed by natural processes, over billions of years! Scientific explanations do not remove the wonder from the world—if anything, they add to it. They reveal how beautifully complex creatures or natural structures were formed over billions of years, and will continue to be formed long after I die. They put into context and, I think, make more stunning my existence—which will last maybe 100 years on a planet that has been here for 4.5 billion years in a universe that has been here for 13.7 billion years.

I now find more meaning in companionship. I think I used to take advantage of my relationships with friends, loved ones, and significant others, because I didn't realize how lucky I am to have all these people around me who care about me. Now, I try my hardest to value and realize the importance of each moment I get with all these wonderful people in my life. Some of the best days of my life have consisted of nothing more than sitting in a backyard with my relatives, strolling around a local park on a sunny day with a friend, or lying in bed on a rainy day with my significant other. These people care deeply about my well-being, as I care deeply about theirs. It is incredible, and I am truly lucky, to be able to experience life with them.

Lastly, my desire to help others has greatly increased. In particular, I have developed a serious personal and professional commitment to helping people in other countries enjoy the freedoms of belief and expression that I enjoy here in the United States. It pains me that people face persecution or legal punishment simply for doubting the prevailing cultural or religious beliefs in which they were raised. One example of this can be seen in the plight of Alexander Aan, the Indonesian civil servant who in June 2012 was sentenced to 30 months in prison for posting about atheism on Facebook. I have tried to assist Alex and, despite all of the challenges he has faced, he has stayed strong, positive, and thankful. It is an incredible testament to the human will.

This is one of the reasons why I love the National Mall. I often come here weeknights—perhaps after a tough day on the job or in life—and reflect on the figures enshrined in history all around me. Lincoln, Jefferson, Washington, Martin Luther King, Jr. ... these people all sacrificed so much— Lincoln and MLK, their *lives*—to help others. I feel I will have wasted my life if I do not strive to meet their standards.

JENNIFER BARDI

EDITOR, *THE HUMANIST* MAGAZINE
WASHINGTON, D.C.

I find tremendous joy in the outdoors. I had picked this spot for the photo because nature comes the closest to giving me a feeling of reverence—what some call a lifting of the spirit. And because modern humans are moving further into private spaces—in which we're still connected, virtually—I think it's important to step out and maintain a connection with nature. Even if it's not a beautiful woodsy environment, I find that being in outside spaces opens me up. It allows for the chance to run into something unexpected, to bump up against others.

Being and feeling connected to other people certainly gives me joy and a sense of mattering. I honestly don't have a spiritual bone in my body but I'm deeply empathetic (yes, commercials can make me cry). If I'm out and I see someone struggling, perhaps, or two friends howling with laughter, I'm often overcome with a sense of attachment. It's the feeling that everybody's going through the same thing or something similar. I'm also inspired by what people are capable of, and can be surprised by the way we behave and misbehave.

This brings me to another source of joy, which is humor. I think of religion as a set of beliefs that look to a divine supernatural force to explain the meaning of human existence, but also as a set of rules to live by that are designed to help us cope with existential anxiety. So for someone who's not religious, the challenge of dealing with these anxieties can be met in part by humor and a healthy dose of the absurd. Albert Camus said that happiness and the absurd are inseparable, which really strikes a chord with me. If we can laugh at ourselves and the situations we find ourselves in, it bodes well for our individual survival.

Do I, as a humanist and an atheist, experience moments of transcendence? Good question. I do occasionally have a kind of metaphysical experience, often when I'm with my husband and kids, where I'm suddenly very aware of my own happiness. Say we've been at the beach all day and we're in the warm car on the way to get ice cream and we're listening to some groovy 70s song on the radio—and I sense (or project?) that my kids are sharing the good feeling, which is imprinting as part of the memory of their childhood. Being aware of such moments is important because, the truth is, life can be very difficult.

I don't think about my own death too much. My dad died prematurely after a high-speed cycling crash, but he lived quite artfully in his 67 years. My great-grandmother made it to 103—was still living on her own in fine health when she died in her sleep. When she turned 100, I was her youngest living relative, so I got to have my picture in the paper with her. I thought it was the greatest thing ever and decided I'd shoot for a century, too. We'll see how it goes.

Being a humanist gives me joy. Sure, it's corny to say you believe in people. But I believe in the idea of *we*—the idea that if we decide to assign a purpose for ourselves on this planet beyond survival, it should be to prosper and to help others prosper. That, for me, is the key to a meaningful life.

Photos: at Muir Woods National Monument, California

FRED EDWORDS
NATIONAL DIRECTOR, UNITED COALITION OF REASON
GREENBELT, MARYLAND

[INTERVIEW] I get joy and meaning from a number of things and, in fact, the same sorts of things that give most people joy and meaning. For, as it turns out, happy people have vital absorbing interests; emotionally significant things they like to do. This was a point the late psychologist Albert Ellis made in connection with his Rational Emotive Behavior Therapy. He advised that one thing a person needs to do to find happiness is get her or himself a vital absorbing interest. It doesn't much matter what it is: it can be stamp collecting, it can be writing a book, it can be pursuing politics. But people need something to get up in the morning for. Because you can't just lie around, relax, and do nothing.

In fact, that whole idea of lying on the beach letting the sun beat down on you, at least for me, gets boring pretty quickly. It can be pleasurable for a short while, yes. But then I'm thinking, okay, now what am I going to do with my time? This isn't the way I want to spend my day. In this context, boredom isn't a state of relaxation, it's a state of agitation. So if I'm not doing anything for long periods of time I can get a bit agitated because I want to be out and about, wanting to see things, wanting to learn something.

For example, when I first went to India, yes, I saw all the usual tourist sites. But I didn't desire to *only* do that. I wanted to know how the people lived. So I hired a taxi to drive me out to the slums of what was then called Bombay, now Mumbai, slums that go on for miles, and take pictures. Likewise, I wanted to see all of the different aspects of Indian life. On a humanist bus tour there, when I was the tour leader, we saw some people out picking cotton in the fields. They were using non-electronic, non-gas operated equipment: a hand operated cotton gin and other such machinery. So we told the bus driver to pull over. Then we all got out and went down to meet with the people in the fields. We talked to them about the cotton and saw up close what they were doing. As you can see, I want to expose myself to new experiences, new people, new learning opportunities.

One particular challenge I enjoy is discovering that something I formerly believed is false. It's often fun to find out that a historical fact or idea that I thought was true isn't, and I go, "Oh wow, that's great." This was my reaction when I gave up traditional religion. When I concluded it wasn't factual, I was excited. But then I did get a little angry, feeling that perhaps I should tell other people. So there's this desire to get the story straight that's built into my nature, then spread the news. There's an intellectual curiosity, the desire to learn and to challenge my earlier assumptions. Thus I've changed my views on a number of important issues over the course of my life and I don't find it at all tragic or problematic.

This may all sound counterintuitive at first. Aren't happiness and meaning supposed to be found in an easy life and good times? Not if you think about how we human beings survived for centuries and centuries, in prehistoric times, ancient times, and so on. For most people over most of that time, life was nasty, brutish, and short. And yet people persevered. They kept having children and they continued on. Many people alive today, if they were suddenly thrust back into that environment, would say that such isn't a life fit to live. Yet people worked through that and struggled and pursued goals and persevered. They did this not because they were particularly virtuous but because we as a species are built for that kind of survival. We're built for struggle. We actually love the struggle. We love the hunt. It's built in.

So when our society manages to solve a lot of the problems, cure the diseases, develop the creature comforts—when we know where our next meal is coming from and have a roof over our head, when we have money and our basic needs are being met, we actually miss the struggle. This is shown in the way we spend our recreational time. We read novels because in order for a novel to tell a story it has to have conflict, it has to have struggle. We get ourselves a vital absorbing interest: get a hobby, get politically active, get involved in social causes. We get into fights with our neighbors or family members—whatever it is that gives us some struggle.

Why does a house cat play with a mouse and not eat it? Because the cat doesn't need to eat the mouse, it isn't hungry, but it still loves to hunt because that's how it survived. Such behavior is built in. Like the cat, we can't take that survival aspect out of our system. If we didn't love the process of surviving, we wouldn't have survived. So love of struggle is what gives life meaning.

Yes, you want to relax and have your highs, and have fun. But these are temporary. What gives life meaning is pursuing some goal where you have to overcome obstacles. And if it's fun and you have triumphs and a few failures, but are enjoying the dance, life becomes exciting, meaningful, powerful, happy.

CHRIS MOONEY
JOURNALIST / AUTHOR / PODCASTER / SCIENCE
COMMUNICATION TRAINER
WASHINGTON, D.C.

[INTERVIEW] I love travel. I love that my job lets me
go all over the world. And it lets me go all over
the world to engage in intellectual activity, which I
find to be the highest, most motivating thing I can
do. I really like the feeling you get when finally
everything clicks, or you're writing a book and
you suddenly know what the answer is.

I believe in secular spirituality, atheist spirituality.
I think atheists have spiritual experiences. It
could be in some kind of understanding achieved
through science or research. It could be in the flow
you achieve while you're doing your intellectual
pursuits. It could be in natural beauty. For a lot of
people it is.

When I was growing up there was a place
that always made me feel like that. I often
go back there and I've even written some of
my books there. It's a house my family has in
Flagstaff, Arizona. It's just gorgeous. It's at the
base of a mountain. And for me it's associated
with the secular worldview because it was my
grandfather's house, and my grandfather is the
reason I'm like this, in the sense that he probably
influenced me more than anybody else. He was
this irascible, Darwinian biologist character. That
was his home. And the place kind of has his ghost
in it. So it all kind of fits.

My philosophy is definitely a *carpe diem* kind
of philosophy. Every moment counts. There's a
kind of dissonance that occurs among very busy
people where they get swept up in their work, and
I'm guilty of that. But what I can help the world
with is making our politics a little bit more sane
by helping more people understand what's true.
And figuring out why people don't like the truth,
whether it's the truth about evolution or whatever
it is. So I've always aimed like an arrow at that
problem. The difficulty is that the closer you look
at it, the harder it gets. But if there's one problem
I want to solve and there's one thing I've gone
a long way towards getting some answers on, it
is that.

REBECCA WATSON
WRITER AND FOUNDER OF *SKEPCHICK*
BUFFALO, NEW YORK

I find joy and meaning in many things, but in particular I find it in all the amazing, breathtaking natural beauty the world has to offer. When I'm close to the place I currently call home, that may be as simple as a bike ride around the beautiful green park system of Buffalo, designed by Frederick Law Olmstead. It may mean standing on the "Hurricane Deck" at Niagara Falls, where I am completely overwhelmed by the power of Bridal Veil Falls crashing around me. Or it may mean a hike around Chestnut Ridge Park, where behind a small waterfall there's an eternal flame fueled by natural gas, which scientists suspect may be produced by deeply submerged deposits of boiling hot shale.

I'm very lucky in that I often have the opportunity to travel further afield. I've been struck dumb floating through dark caverns filled with glowworms, and felt my heart in my throat as I leapt off rocks into a crystal clear Mediterranean. I'm regularly awed by sunsets over just about any beach, but my favorite may have been the pink and orange horizons I saw in Malaysia as I sat on a weathered log with a beer in my hand and a friend by my side.

Friends, of course, would be my other main source of joy—old friends from kindergarten as well as the new friends I meet every time I travel. My friends helped me establish and run Boston Skeptics in the Pub (and they continue to run it today), and my friends helped me launch and grow Skepchick. org. My friends gave me their couches when I didn't have a bed, and their beers when I didn't have a bank account. My friends encourage me to keep going when I want to give up. They push me to keep exploring when I think I've seen enough. They bring out the best in me and forgive the worst. They teach me every day how to find the joy in life.

CARA SANTA MARIA
SCIENCE COMMUNICATOR / WRITER / CO-HOST AND PRODUCER, *TAKEPART LIVE* ON PIVOT TV
LOS ANGELES, CALIFORNIA

[INTERVIEW] I lead a pretty calm, simple life that I try to fill with love and appreciation for the beauty of nature. I'm not the kind of person who needs to do things for the adrenaline rush. I would describe myself as something of a homebody. I love to stay home and read. I also love my dog, Killer. He's always there for me and he brings me a lot of comfort. I love science. I love my job. I love my friends and my family. I try to find joy in really simple things. I'm definitely the kind of person who doesn't need a lot of external stimulation. There's a lot going on in my mind all the time—I actually take antidepressants because I struggle with mental illness. So I find it necessary to maintain a calm, serene environment. I also don't drink or smoke. My biggest vice is Coca-Cola. I'm not the kind of person who goes out to "da club."

As a science communicator, it's exciting to be able to learn so much about the cosmos. When I look up at the stars, I find so much meaning—I'm humbled. When I was in academia focusing on psychology and neuroscience, I often peered inward and felt awe and wonder at our inner worlds. But science is everywhere. It's in everything. Science is the way we think about the world. It's the way we interact with nature, with our reality. And that kind of "religious" experience

that a lot of people might describe—what they might call spirituality, which to me is such a bullshit term—it's absolutely everywhere.

Before I studied science in school, I studied vocal jazz, and I used to sing often in church. I would get goose bumps when I heard sacred music. I was always told, "It's the spirit running through you. That's God running through you." I think there was this "Aha" moment one day when I thought, "No, I just really like music. I have an emotional response to music whether it's sacred or secular." At the time when those songs were written, that was the prevailing thought—it's just what people wrote about. The music is beautiful regardless of the subject matter. I think once I made that realization, things came into focus for me, and I still really love sacred music.

I'm super nerdy and I have a lot of nerdy tattoos. I have the Berlin specimen of *Archaeopteryx lithographica*, a transitional fossil, on my arm. My most recent tattoo is a quote from Carl Sagan, "We are a way for the cosmos to know itself." It really resonates with me because I don't believe in God or any sort of cosmic consciousness. I don't think there's some pseudoscientific energy source running around controlling things.

We are made of atoms that were created in the explosions of the stars, and we ourselves have evolved this incredible ability to contemplate our place in the universe. Since we can contemplate ourselves and we are made of the stuff of the cosmos, then by transitive properties we are a way for the cosmos to know itself. Without us, it can't know itself. Of course, that puts us in this very special position.

I'm not saying we're necessarily the only ones. There may be other forms of intelligent life that we haven't come across and we don't even know about. There may be whole civilizations that have risen and fallen. But those of us with that very special gift should respect it. There's so much beauty out there that doesn't have the ability to contemplate itself. Since we can, I think we should really honor that and reflect on our place in the cosmos in a reverent way. That doesn't mean believing in God—it means really trying to understand the science.

LEIGHANN LORD

STAND-UP COMEDIAN / WRITER / ACTRESS
QUEENS, NEW YORK

Having the ability and freedom to follow my dream brings me joy, and that dream is being a working, professional stand-up comedian. It has allowed me to do my favorite things in life: traveling, writing, performing, making people laugh, sleeping in, and staying out of the corporate cubicle. Pressed particleboard makes me quite cranky.

I was lucky to have parents who encouraged and supported my dreams. My Mom said, "Do it, so you don't ever have to look back and say, 'I wish I had.'" My Dad said, "Do it. You'll be good at anything that lets you talk... a lot." For me, that narrowed it down to becoming lawyer or stand-up comedian. I chose the latter since I am not a great standardized-test taker.

Stand-up comedy has allowed me to work all over the world. I had a passport before I had a driver's license. I've had the thrill of performing in some of the most beautiful theaters. I've also told jokes in a hurricane-ravaged, third-world country while standing atop a flat bed truck, illuminated only by car headlights. It ain't always glamorous, but it is always interesting.

I've felt the rush of receiving a standing ovation. There's absolutely nothing like it. You can't ask for one. Well, you can, but it's really tacky. A standing ovation is an audience saying, "Thanks for the joy, now let us give some back to you."

I've also been humbled by that audience member who has sought me out after a show to hug me, shake my hand, look me in the eye, and tell me they've just lost their job, or a loved one, or they've been diagnosed with cancer; and more than anything in the world they needed to laugh, and I helped them do that. It's very much like the feeling I got on September 13, 2001, when I walked into a New York comedy club and found people who, in the face of fear and uncertainty, chose to avail themselves of the healing power of laughter. It is no small thing to know that pursing my joy in life has brought joy to others. Does it get any better than that? I think not.

Stand-up comedy has immersed me in the soup of human diversity. I have met people from many cultures, ethnicities, nationalities, economic backgrounds, and houses (we can't all be from Gryffindor, now can we?). And while our differences are way funnier than our similarities, it is the latter that is most important. Tragic farm accidents aside, we've each got ten fingers, ten toes, one head, one heart. We are an awesomely talented, yet troubled little species that suffers from taking itself a tad too seriously. Luckily, I can help.

Photos: performing at Comic Strip Live, New York

PENN JILLETTE
ILLUSIONIST / MAGICIAN
LAS VEGAS, NEVADA

[INTERVIEW] I've got a bunch of followers on Twitter and many of them are believers and probably every day, somebody writes something like, "I'm sorry that religious people treated you so badly that you became an atheist." And it's really quite the contrary. Religious people have treated me wonderfully my whole life. My dad was a Christian his whole life and died a Christian and he was wonderful to me. We had this perfect, loving relationship and as I became an atheist and a more outspoken atheist, we would discuss it. He would pray for me. My dad would say stuff like, "After I die, I'm going to work so hard to get you, your mother and sister into heaven, but I will do it." Even my pastor, when I became atheist, was very, very kind. And my whole life, even at the Penn & Teller show, many, many, many, many, many, many fans were religious and many of them were not oblivious to the fact that we're atheists— and yet, after the show, they showed nothing but kindness. I mean, there are a few isolated incidents where people were unpleasant to me, but the vast majority, I mean if you rounded it off, everybody who is religious has been nice to me.

I don't think anything gives your life joy and meaning. I think your life simply has joy and meaning. I think it's built in. It's so odd to me that people need meaning in life beyond the meaning of life. There's a kind of sadness in religion. When someone talks to me about their love of God or their love of Jesus Christ, all I hear is that they believe that the love of their friends and family is not enough and I see that as a slap in the face. My parents are dead now but I have a wife and

two children. I don't know how one can look into the eyes of their children and have that not be enough. I don't know why that isn't enough meaning for anyone. Having children, having a wife, having a family floods me with more joy than I could possibly need in life and more meaning than I could ever covet. The love for my children, the love for my parents and the love for my friends, is the end in itself.

The meaning *is* life. It's like asking someone who's sitting in a banquet, where are you going to get the food? Well it's right here in front of you, motherfucker. I'm just filled with that and I don't even need to give you that whole list. My son is eight. One moment of touching his hand. One moment thinking of him. One moment with my hand on his head. One moment looking into his eyes. One moment hearing his voice call me "daddy" and there is more than enough meaning and more than enough joy for infinite lifetimes. I don't know how anyone can experience the kind of love that we have in our lives and not find joy and meaning. For those who don't have strong families—there's still life. I don't know how a deep breath through one's nose or looking at a sunset or eating Jell-O or any of the joys we experience on a daily basis—I don't know how that's not joy, and meaning and plenty of both.

Awe and wonder is as full and human and natural and constant as a heartbeat and by the way, the heartbeat causes that as well. Just the thought of a heartbeat, gives you awe and wonder. It's a silly statement for someone to say that they look up

into the dark night sky and see awe and wonder. You didn't feel it before you got out of your house? What the fuck were you, high?

I was very close to my mom and dad, and people would find out I was an atheist and they would say, like throwing down this gauntlet, "Well, you wait till your mom and dad die! You know, you'll find that you need a God then." The cruelty of that is astonishing. My mom took a long while to die. She was paralyzed, she suffered a lot and then she died. She was the closest person to me in the world. I am a real mama's boy. And I found a huge amount of comfort in my atheism. I really can't imagine the amount of pain I would have felt if I believed in God. The idea that I would have to find a way that an omniscient, omnipresent, omnipotent, loving God chose for my mom to suffer in a plan that I didn't understand. Yup, that's a plan I don't understand, I'll give you that. I don't understand why a God would choose to have my mother suffer. That's inconceivable to me. The atheist idea that my mom suffered, not because of a God that made that choice, but because of random universe, just the way the cookie crumbles, as Mom would say—there's a great deal of comfort in that. There's a great deal of comfort that no amount of praying could have helped her. There's a great deal of comfort in knowing that nothing she did in her life brought this on her. All of that is comforting. And even with my mom gone, the memory of her love is still in my heart, and that gives me more than enough joy and meaning for the rest of my life and my children's lives.

TELLER
ILLUSIONIST / MAGICIAN
LAS VEGAS, NEVADA

[INTERVIEW] When I was a kid, my parents bought 16 acres of rocky woodland in Bucks County, Pennsylvania and we used to go up on weekends and camp in a little cabin my father built. On warm afternoons, sometimes after a rain when the leaves were fragrant and dripping, my mother used to take me up the deer path to her "sitting rock." She'd seat me next to her and tell me to listen, just listen. The wind would move the trees. Animals would skitter and stir. Bees would buzz by. And I'd feel the eternal in the momentary. It still gives me shivers to remember it. Who needs a church if you have a sitting rock?

When I was nine or ten, my parents thought it would be worthwhile for me to sample what it would be like in a church (my mother's side was Methodist). So I went to Sunday school for a year or two. But when the time came to join the church, which everyone in my Sunday school class was doing, my parents said, "No, you don't do that now. You wait till you're a grownup to make that decision." I thought it was very interesting way to educate me, to let me get a taste of religion, but not let me get sucked into it. It was rather like strapping Odysseus to the ship's mast so he could hear the Sirens' song without diving overboard.

In Sunday school, I saw how logic can be used to mislead, to ensnare intellectual kids. For example, they teach: (1) A sacrifice is a traditional way of appeasing God. (2) Man's sin got so great

that finally God needed a human victim of utter purity. (3) Therefore God considerately provided a human victim to satisfy his own craving. The logic of the progression disguises the fact that the underlying ideas are all daffy. Providing your own sacrifice to mollify your own rage? Isn't there a psychiatric diagnosis for that disorder?

The idea of atheism sort of floated vaguely in the background for many, many, many years. But I don't think I named myself an atheist until I knew Penn. I just didn't care. But he helped me learn to care. Somebody once asked him what depressed him most. He said, "How short life is." Atheism makes you treasure every moment.

I have a craving to be in touch with the eternal—that sense that I felt when sitting as a child with my mother on the rock. What supplies it for me is the arts. I was a Latin and Greek student and the idea that somebody who'd been dead for 2,000 years could sing again directly to me was thrilling. These words lived when humans died and empires fell. Horace called poetry, "A monument more lasting than bronze." The maxim "*ars longa, vita brevis*," ("art is long, live is short") is one I live by.

That was the idea behind the tombstone I wrote about in *How to Play in Traffic*. We have at Forest Lawn Burbank a Penn & Teller grave marker. On it, is the Three of Clubs and "IS THIS YOUR CARD?" I love the idea that as long as the cemetery is

there—even long after we're dead—we can provide fans with the denouement to a card trick.

In the theater you create a moment, but in that moment, there is a touch, a twinkle of eternity. And not just eternity, but community. When you laugh in the theater it's because you *get* something that's been left unsaid. It's what I love about working silent. If I can do something that conveys an idea without stating it and the audience laughs or gasps in response, I know they are with me and with one another. That connection is a sense of life for me. And the community that arises around artistic events is sensual and intimate. In *The Symposium* Plato talks about artistic types giving "birth in beauty," and I have to say that artistic collaboration is at the top of my list of what makes me feel alive.

I also think religious people miss out on the tangible, sensual pleasure of helping others. They think when they help a blind person cross the street, it's pleasing to a god and earns them a reward. If I help somebody, it's erotic. I get all blushy and hot, and sometimes have to hide the rush of blood or the tears, so that I don't embarrass the person I'm helping. There's something fantastically sexy about helping somebody in need. I'm placing a bit of me into a bit of them.

GRETA CHRISTINA
WRITER / SPEAKER
SAN FRANCISCO, CALIFORNIA

So there's kind of a weird story about these photos.

The day these photos were taken was the day I found out I had cancer. I literally had gotten the news about the cancer thirty seconds before Chris knocked on my door.

I considered canceling—but I'd already had to cancel on Chris once, not even two weeks earlier. Ironically, because my father died the day we were first supposed to shoot. And this project was important to me. So I put on my best game face, and went ahead with the shoot.

I didn't tell Chris. I hadn't had a chance yet to tell Ingrid, and with all due respect to Chris, I wasn't about to tell some photographer I'd never met that I'd just been diagnosed with cancer before I told my wife. So again—game face. We walked around my neighborhood looking at street art, and we sat in my backyard, and we talked about joy and purpose and the meaning of life when there is no God and death is final, and every time I looked into the camera lens, I was thinking, "Cancer. Cancer. Cancer."

It was, to say the least, a very strange day. Especially when Ingrid showed up to join me on the shoot: I knew about the cancer, but she didn't know, and I didn't want to tell her until after Chris had left, so I had to do the shoot with her, knowing that I was about to tell her this enormous horrible news, and sitting with the knowledge that she didn't yet know. But it also gave the photo shoot an intensity, a poignancy. Sitting with Ingrid in our home; talking about what gives my life value; framing shots that might capture part of the essence of that life—all not knowing how much of it I'd have left—put a sharp focus on that day, even as it made it deeply surreal. And even in the moment, it seemed like some sort of metaphor: we have so little control over what happens to us in our lives, but we can choose how to respond to it. I chose to handle this dreadful day, this dreadfully bizarre day, by biting the bullet and moving forward with the things that matter to me.

I got lucky. The cancer was caught early; it was entirely treated with surgery; I am now cancer-free. But I don't think I'll ever be able to look at these photos without thinking of the strangeness of that day—and without thinking, not only of how beautiful life is, but how fragile.

Following page: Christina and her partner Ingrid with their backyard "Great Wall of China"

239

I DO BELIEVE
BY MICHELLE RHEA

"I do believe in the religion of justice, of kindness. I believe in humanity.
I do believe that usefulness is the highest possible form of worship...
I care nothing about supernatural myths and mysteries, but I do care for human beings."

— *Robert Green Ingersoll*

I believe it is good to be kind,
to nurture compassion and empathy,
to strive for civility,
and to cultivate joy in my life
and in the lives of others.

I believe in doing no harm
to myself, to other people,
or to animals.

I believe in personal responsibility
for my thoughts,
my words,
and my actions.

I believe in honor and integrity
and the ethic of doing what is right
just because it is right
and not for some rumored reward.

I believe this life has the meaning
we choose to create,
and that eternal existence
could not make it more precious
than it already is.

I believe we have no gods to credit
or devils to blame
but have only each other to turn to,
to love, to aid, and to cherish.

I do not believe we are fallen,
but I do believe we can rise.

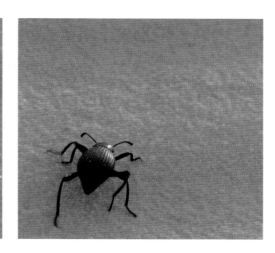

ACKNOWLEDGEMENTS

Many people have contributed to make this project a reality. In addition to the 100 subjects who opened up their lives, and welcomed me into their homes to share what brings joy & meaning to them, there were many more who helped along the way:

Firstly, I want to thank my exceptionally talented brother **Peter Johnson**, without whom this project never would have happened.

My father **Kenneth Johnson**, mother **Edith Gower & Margaret Doughty** for always being there and supporting me. The rest of my supportive family: **Nancy White, Tim McVey, Carolyn Johnson & Timo, Bruce E.H. Johnson & Sandra Davis, Cynthia Johnson, Paige Miller, Marta Johnson & Johann Rocholl, Winslow Johnson, Russell Johnson, Jordan Wylie, St. John & Lauren Johnson, Sarajane Johnson & Arthur Goldberg, David Goldberg, Marc & Chrissy Goldberg, Reg Gower, Jody Gower Lavrich, Kimberly Gower Dallow** and **Cindy Guy.**

Gordy French for being the greatest friend anyone could ever ask for.

Xavier Montecel and **Alex Corbitt**

Ken Bloom

Cesar Rodriguez, Josh Ellis, Kenneth Kantor, Peter Filichia, Bob Sixsmith, Andy Propst and **David Schmittou.**

Andy Lefkowitz, Erik Campano, Helena Guzik and **Tracie Harris,** for all their help.

Scott Citron of **Scott Citron Design** for helping with Lightroom photo editing. Thanks also to **Erika K. Hammer** of **Ten-2-Ten Photography.**

Jennifer Perito, Adam Casini, Alex Rodriguez, Liza Michael & Rachel Allison for modeling for the design mockups.

Doug Beeferman, San Francisco, CA; **Delane Bertsch**, Los Angeles, CA; **Jacob Colling**, Madison, WI; **BJ Kramer**, New York, NY; **Aaron Scheinberg**, Cambridge, MA; **Dana Weber**, Seattle, WA; for assisting with various shoots and interviews.

John Winson & Laura Lee Johnson, & (the late) **Foster**, Boston, MA, and **Nick & Jasper French**, London, UK for hosting me during my travels.

The staff and team at **Kickstarter** for creating a platform to make this dream a reality.

Arlo J. Pignotti of AJ Processing in Austin, TX for transcriptions. In addition: **Elisa Perkins, Chris Baker** and **Joe Zamecki.**

Edward Starkman at StarPrint Brokers.

David Diskin & Caralee Hickey.

Special thanks to **Anita M. Barnard** and **Michelle Rhea** for their poetry.

IN ADDITION:

Doug Coker & Otis, Seattle, WA; **David Corrini**, New York, NY; **Steven DiMarzo**, Syracuse, NY; **Andrew Goldman**, Rochester, NY; **Roger Swonger**, Cincinnati, OH; **Tim Shin & Stephanie Moore**, Austin, TX; The cast and crew of **The Atheist Experience**, Austin, TX; **Erik Gerard**, Los Angeles, CA; **Craig Jorczak**, Los Angeles, CA; **Aramael Andres Pena-Alcantara**, New York, NY; **Comic Strip Live**, New York, NY; **Central Restaurant**,

Washington, DC; **Elias Montilla** of Tryst Coffee, Washington, DC; **Metropolitan Ballroom**, Charlotte, NC; **Adam Isaak**, Buffalo, NY; **Andrew Harrison**, Rochester, NY; **Herman Yiu, CPA**, New York, NY; **Rick Steves**, Seattle, WA; **Stephen and Coops**, London, UK; **Juliette Meinrath, Michelle Blankenship & Laura Gianino; Rand Russell**, Oxford, England; **Robert Ashby**, of the British Humanist Association; **Glenn Alai**, of Penn and Teller; **Maureen Berejka**, Cold Spring Harbor, NY; **Maitreya Padukone, DMD PC**, New York, NY; **Dr. Bruce Champagne, MD**, New York, NY.

Image of cosmic microwave background: WMAP #121238; Credit: **NASA / WMAP Science Team** (2012). Image of Harry Blackstone, Sr. poster; Oriental Nights; Credit: **Erie Lithograph Company**, Erie, PA (1918). Shelley Segal's guitar courtesy **Maton Guitars Australia**. Portrait of Christopher Hitchens and Carol Blue painted by **Anthony Palliser**.

Michael Lapa & Charlene Cote, James Cocciardi & Nadine Cardinal, Cameron MacLeod, Steven Lapidus & Matthew Hays, and **Erin Grainger & Matthew Stebbins.**

The incredibly talented **Will Curry** and the 25th anniversary national tour of **Les Misérables.**

Anne Klaeysen and the **New York Society for Ethical Culture.**

Michael Payton and the **Centre for Inquiry-Canada**: www.centreforinquiry.ca

Concordia University, Montreal, QC

American Airlines

Author photo by **Gary LosHuertos.**

KICKSTARTER THANK-YOUS

Damian Abbott
Peter Abrahamsen
Sarah Maude Adams, MSW
Jorge Alagón
Janel Andersen
J. Andersen
Brandee Anderson
James Anderson
Doug Anton
Maggie Ardiente
Ian Ashman
James Auburn
Michael Backs
Marcus Baker
Gail Baymiller
Isone Beach
Raquel Benitez
Rada Bittner-Rozenberg
Andy Bloch
Ken Bloom
Peter Bollwerk
Michael Borland
Todd Allen Bowers
Christopher Bradey
Donald & Erin Breda
Fred Bremmer
Dustin Brewer
Robert Bull
Brendan Burke
Arturo Calvillo
Ellen Carter
Jake Cassidy
Michael Cawthon
Andrew Champion
Kalel Chase
Laron Cheek
Robert Clarke
Keith Collura
Laura Cooper
Michael Covarrubias
Glenn Crouch

Richard Daily, MD
Kathryn Daves
Alan Davidson
Barbara Davis
Kevin Davis
Stewart Dean
Julien Declercq
Joe L. Decocq
David DeGroote
Brian Delaney
Joseph Desy
Steven DiMarzo
David Diskin
Andy Downard
Mark Duyvesteyn
Scott Ecelberger
J Corey Edmonds
Steve Farmer
Belinda Fernandez
Gustavo Ferreyro
Ken Finklea
Alison Flynn
Michel Forest
James Freeman
Gordy French
Benoit Fries
Cinthia Fulton
Blake Furman
Jason Galeon
Brian Gaston
Hans Gerwitz
Douglas Gillis
Arthur Goldberg
Gary Gordon
Andrew Gradisher
Erin Grainger
Joshua Green
Jerwin Mark Llagas Guillermo
George Hadley
John Hall
Penelope Hamilton

Matthew Hargus
Christopher Harlow
Chris Harrop
Joanne Head
Randall Heath
Allison Hofmann
Alex Honnold
Jeff Houser
Stephen Steb Howard
Jeff & Bonnie Howden
Mark F. Hryniuk
Otis Isadog
Bo Jeanes
Lauren Johnson
Marta Noble Johnson
Russell Johnson
Sarajane Johnson
St. John Johnson
Kate Jones
Ramanan Kandasamy
Jess Kaufman
Lisa Kelley
Craig Kennedy
Jörg Klausewitz, M.Sc.
Johan Kolmodin
Jeanne Koploy
Michael Lapa
Gertrude LaPrune
Hans Christian Larssen
J. M. Lee
Caroline Legault-Forest
Christi & Joel Legawiec
Brian Leodler
Michael Lewis
George Lichman
Auston Lind
Jim Lippard
Chuck Litzell
Adam Malinoski
Roy Manterfield
Anthony Marchesano

Megan Matthews
Tim McCollough
Erik McKee
Shon Bryr McLean
Timothy McVey
Matthew Medina
Courtney Meehan
Daniel Melin
Alejandro Paiz Meschler
Lisa Milewski
Thomas Mokwa
Xavier Montecel
Kristin Muller
Bob Munsil
D. Shane Myers
Matt Naumann
Derrick Niemann
Eric O'Connor
Sam K. Owens III
Brian Ozinga
Michael Payne
Michael Pelikan
Justin Ponsor
Sven Pride
Nick Proctor
Stacie Rasmussen
Michelle Rhea
Nick Robertson
Eric Robinson
Victor Rodrigues
William Roe
Sandra Rogers
Brian Rubinow
Daniel Sachse
Dan Sadro
Sam Salerno
Allan Sanceau
Lyle Sanders
Stefano Saykaly
David Schilling
Ryan Schneider

Tako Schotanus
Christian Schudoma
Erin & Marty Schutte
Eric Scott
William Sharpe
Julian Shelton
Bryan Sisto
Jeremiah Smith
Todd Smith
Matthew Stebbins
Michael Sternberg
Jan Suchanek
Joseph Sullivan
Steve Sullivan
Jakub Swiatczak
Alex Szeto
Carol Thomas
Mathias Thylander
Danny Tosolini
Bruce Tripp
Greggari Tucker
Jasper Turcotte
Paul Unseld
Kurt Van Etten
Steve VanHorn
Katie Vice
Benjamin Waggoner
Timothy Wascoe
Justin Wells
Cory B. White
Hanne Winter
Chantal Yacavone
Tim & Kathy Zebo-Hjelle
Steven Zimmerman

In memory of
Jeremy Michael Kelley

Additional thanks to all
others who supported this
book through Kickstarter.

ALPHABETICAL INDEX OF NAMES

ABOUT THE PHOTOGRAPHER

CHRIS JOHNSON is a New York-based photographer and filmmaker. He received his undergraduate degree in film production (along with a minor in religious studies) from Concordia University in Montreal, Quebec. His photography has been seen in *The New York Times*.

Apart from his own film and photographic work, he has also collaborated with artists and directors in various roles and capacities from assistant director and stage manager, for theatre, film, and print. His work in art direction and production design can be seen in the films *Les Mercredis de Rose* by acclaimed Quebecois director Guylaine Dionne and *The Pen and the Sword*, produced in part by the National Film Board of Canada.

Chris is the recipient of the Kodak Award for Excellence in Filmmaking as well as the B.F. Lorenzetti Scholarship for Excellence in Filmmaking.

Website: www.christophergowerjohnson.com